Pageantry

ON THE

SHAKESPEAREAN STAGE

ALICE V. GRIFFIN

COLLEGE AND UNIVERSITY PRESS
New Haven, Connecticut

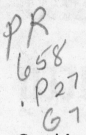

With the permission of the publishers, Ginn and Company, quotations from Shakespeare are from the 1936 edition of *The Complete Works of Shakespeare,* edited and copyright by George Lyman Kittredge.

REPRINTED WITH PERMISSION OF TWAYNE PUBLISHERS, INC. BY COLLEGE AND UNIVERSITY PRESS, PAPERBACK DIVISION

Designed by Fred Kleeberg

MANUFACTURED IN THE UNITED STATES OF AMERICA

TO ERNEST HUNTER WRIGHT

Contents

Illustrations

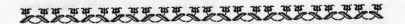

Introduction

THE APPEAL of public spectacle is timeless. Today, the marching men and decorated floats of an inaugural or Mardi Gras parade hold the same attraction which drew throngs to the Roman triumphs and to the Elizabethan royal entries. In Roman times, the declining drama took on more and more the aspect of these public spectacles until it degenerated into mere exhibition. In Shakespeare's day, the public display was likewise drawn upon, not to supplant a dying art, but to enrich a developing one. These popular ceremonies celebrating a sovereign or foreign ambassador or Lord Mayor provided the chief spectacle in the lives of the citizens who filled most of the space at the public playhouses. It was an easy matter for dramatists to duplicate upon the huge platform stage at the Globe or the Rose or the Swan just such royal and civic processions which in real life attracted crowds of spectators to the streets, to the windows, and to the very rooftops. As a feature of the public ceremonies, shows (or pageants) presented political and moral themes by means of living actors mounted upon floats, decorated landmarks, and city gates. When the themes of such "street shows" were carried over to the stage, part of the original technique of presentation was preserved, sometimes inadvertently. At other times, however, playwrights achieved subtle and artistic effects by intentionally employing devices resembling the pageant. In addition, an Elizabethan dramatist might color his dialogue with allusions and imagery concerning the vivid public spectacles.

This study attempts to analyze the influence on the Elizabethan drama of the most popular forms of public display—the procession, pageant, and progress entertainment. The non-Shakespearean plays considered here have been limited, except for a few references, to those written in Elizabeth's reign. A thorough investigation has been made of all extant plays presented from 1581 to 1603, when both pageant and drama reached their heights as purely public entertainments, to decline later, as the private masque and theatre increased in importance. Although a monarch might on occasion endure for six hours the "pageants of delight," the less hardy reader will be entertained here with only representative examples. The appendix lists the events which are referred to in the text and gives the most accessible printed sources. An extensive chronological survey has not been attempted. Historical treatments of the form already exist in two fine works to which this present study is indebted—Robert Withington's *English Pageantry* on the history and development of the pageant, and George Kernodle's *From Art to Theatre* on the *tableaux vivants* and show architecture in relation to art and the Renaissance physical stage. The present undertaking is concerned with a comparative examination of the public entertainments and the public drama. It is hoped that this new perspective may reveal a fuller significance in many scenes and a richer reading in numerous passages in Elizabethan drama, and may contribute to the appreciation and enjoyment of Shakespeare in the study and upon the stage.

I should like to express my gratitude to Columbia University for the generous fellowship which made this work possible and to the members of the Department of English, especially Professors Oscar James Campbell, Alfred Harbage, and Maurice Valency, who made my study so rewarding. For their helpful assistance I also should like to thank Professor Ernest Shepard of George Washington University, Mr. Willard Webb of the Library of Congress, and Dr. Louis Wright, Dr. James Mc-Manaway, and Miss Dorothy Mason of the Folger Shakespeare Library.

A. S. V.

Hunter College
New York City
October, 1950

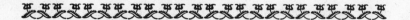

CHAPTER ONE

Entries and Triumphs

ON STAGE

> Many a time and oft
> Have you climb'd up to walls and battlements,
> To tow'rs and windows, yea, to chimney tops,
> Your infants in your arms, and there have sat
> The livelong day, with patient expectation,
> To see great Pompey pass the streets of Rome.
>
> I, i, 42 ff.

THIS PICTURE of a public reception in *Julius Caesar* was not confined to ancient history in the minds of the men and women of Shakespeare's audience. They too, had lined London's streets and watched from windows and rooftops to see a spectacular royal entry or Lord Mayor's Show. When King James I rode through the city in celebration of his coronation, Thomas Dekker reported that "the streets seemde to be paued with men; stalles instead of rich wares were set out for children; open casements fild up with women."[1] Members of all classes and occupations swarmed to gaze at the splendor which transformed their thoroughfares not only at coronations, but at processions of the sovereign to Parliament

or on departure from or return to London, receptions for
foreign ambassadors, and annual installations of the Lord
Mayor.[2] In the crowds which he depicts at public celebrations,
whether of Roman or English history, Shakespeare places
carpenters, cobblers, draymen, ladies, matrons, oyster wenches, nobles and nurses. Such townspeople might applaud the
marches of costumed maskers through the streets, or parades
of tournament contestants into the lists; from the banks of
the Thames, Londoners might cheer a sham battle between
vessels trimmed to represent English merchants and pirates,
or might admire a formation of gorgeously decorated barges
honoring the ruler or the Lord Mayor. These same citizens
made up the majority at the public playhouses. A playwright
concerned with his audience's tastes needed no heightened
perception to realize the attraction which public spectacle
held for most of the penny-payers facing the stage.

The age was one of glitter and bright colors, the vivid reds
and blues and yellows which a painter might turn to after a
long period of working with muted, somber tones. Perhaps
Renaissance England chose a brilliant decor because of the new
appreciation of external beauty; perhaps it wore a brave state
out of memory at the dark times that had been and out of
apprehension that they might come again. On occasions of
public celebration, this decoration was most manifest in two
forms—the kaleidoscopic procession and the still-life tableaux.

Through the streets moved the splendid parade, its participants riding ornately-caparisoned horses or marching before
and behind the honored personage, most resplendent upon
horseback or in a canopied litter. The bright costumes were
of velvet, silk and satin, the men's decorated with massive
gold chains, the ladies' sparkling with emeralds, rubies and
diamonds. The line bristled with staves, lances, banners and
other emblems of office carried by the official participants. At
the head of the procession marched the trumpeters and her-

alds to announce the approaching spectacle, while "wild men" or "whifflers" capered about with torches or swords to clear a path through the crowd of spectators. A rich setting for the parade, the houses which walled the streets displayed colored banners and hung tapestries and painted cloths from their windows. Mounted upon the elaborately-decorated landmarks along the route, living actors formed tableaux which honored the occasion. (See Plate I).

The *tableaux vivants,* or street shows, developed from mere decorations to allegorical pageants. In the Middle Ages, the larger cities staged triumphal marches, royal entries, and religious and civic processions which featured the carrying of symbolic images and the decoration of landmarks along the way. It was customary on such occasions to trim the cities' gates and arches, whereon musicians or singing children were sometimes stationed.[3] The responsibility for the civic welcomes fell naturally upon the guilds, which furthered the use of representation and symbolism by displaying figures of patron saints and emblematic animals. In London in 1298, for instance, the Fishmongers celebrated the victory of Edward I at Falkirk by displaying gilded sturgeons and silver salmons. The city pageants likewise applied to the celebration at hand characters and situations from history and from the Bible. Thus the guild-sponsored mystery plays and pageants might utilize the same costumes and properties. At his entry after Agincourt in 1415, Henry V was hailed by the twelve apostles in one pageant and the Old Testament prophets in another. At the cross in Cheapside, "the archangelic and angelic multitude . . . sent forth . . . *minae* of gold, with boughs of laurel" upon Henry's head, to signify divine approval of his succession to the throne. Ironically enough, a mechanical angel in the pageant may have been the same one used earlier at the celebration of the coronation of Richard II, later deposed by Henry V's father.[4] While the less elaborate exhibits could be carried along in the procession, these shows presented to Henry V were mounted upon fixed stages, in accordance with the growing practice of placing the *tableaux vivants* on the city gates, on especially constructed street stages, or on London landmarks.[5]

The first elaborately allegorical devices in England were presented in 1432 to honor the royal entry of Henry VI into London. At this young King's coronation in Paris, the displays had included exhibitions of the Nine Worthies of history, and of Fame in her triumphal chariot. In London, when Henry and his procession halted at a decorated conduit, they saw a *tableau vivant* depicting a boy king surrounded by personified abstractions of monarchial virtues—Mercy, Truth and Clemency. In another pageant, the grocers' guild displayed a "flourishing paradise" which represented the prosperous city; a third device graphically demonstrated by means of a genealogical tree Henry's rightful succession to the thrones of France and England.

The influence of these pageants is reflected in themes and techniques in Elizabethan drama; the procession, quite adaptable to physical representation in its own form on the large, bare platform stage, becomes the chief means for supplying the spectacle so popular with the audience. In almost every play produced in London's popular theatres of the eighties, the "big" scene is one of a spectacular procession. In that decade, among the outstanding stage displays were the coronation in *The Famous Victories of Henry the Fifth*, the triumphal entries in *Tamburlaine* and *The Spanish Tragedy*, the progress of the ruler to the university in *Friar Bacon and Friar Bungay*, and the parades of personified abstractions in *Faustus* and *The Three Lords and Three Ladies of London*. As it grew in popularity, the chronicle play persistently sought visual appeal by staging processions which had been described in detail by historians. These plays abound in military marches, triumphal parades, royal entries, and funeral processions. The last-named, while serving the practical purpose of clearing the stage of bodies, provided ceremony as well, an effect which opens 1 *Henry VI,* where Shakespeare stages the funeral procession of Henry V as described in Hall's *Chronicle.*[6] The processional entries of a sovereign or hero after a military triumph or for coronation might be staged to provide visual appeal, to increase moments of tension, or to represent symbolically the height of fortune of a proud hero who was later to fall; sometimes the stage procession was muted for special effects of contrast.

Although perhaps more handsome than fine, the color and movement of the royal entries were reproduced by the chronicle plays with the same attempt at super-realistic detail and elaboration of splendor which characterize our historical motion pictures. One of the highlights of *Edward I,* an early English chronicle play by George Peele, was the entry of Edward to his coronation:

Enter the nine lordes of Scotland, with their nine pages, Gloster, Sussex, King Edward in his sute of Glasse; Queene Elinor, Queene Mother, the King and Queene vnder a Canopie.

iii, 683 ff.

It will be noted that some twenty-three persons are called for, in accordance with what seemed to be the general practice in staging processions—bringing on "as many as can be." Since most of the roles for such ensemble scenes demanded no more talent than the ability to wear a costume, carry a piece of property, and keep fairly well in line, the required personnel could be recruited not only from among the sharers, hired actors and boys, but also the playhouse workmen. That such a considerable number of persons did "fill the scene" is revealed in W. W. Greg's study of extant "plots" or outlines of stage entrances, for several plays of the Admiral's Company.

These plots called for twenty-five persons to appear in *The Battle of Alcazar,* and about twenty-seven in *Tamar Cam,* presented c. 1602, which utilized every actor and attendant available for its splendid final entries and tableau. The processions were generally staged after the play was well under way, when the actors' more manually-inclined associates were free to serve Thespis. The plot for *Frederick and Basilea,* for instance, calls for theatrical attendants to act as Lords in scene viii, and gatherers (admission collectors) to represent soldiers in scene xviii.[7]

While the actors provided the movement, the costumes and properties furnished the color for stage spectacles. Thus the playing companies' wardrobes were extensive and elaborate. The "suit of glass" which Edward wore in Peele's play was no doubt made especially for the occasion, as were the ambassadors' outfits in John Webster's *The White Devil* and the knights' costumes in the Shakespeare-Fletcher *Henry VIII.* The inventories of Philip Henslowe for the Lord Admiral's Men list such regalia as "Tamberlanes breches of crymson vellvet," "Harrye the v velvet gowne," and "Harye the v satten dublet, layd with gowld lace." Perhaps figuring in stage processions were the following properties recorded by Henslowe:

j longe sorde [perhaps for a wiffler], iij trumpettes and a drum, viij lances, j globe & j golden scepter, j wooden canepie, ij coffenes, j poopes miter, iij Imperial crownes, j playne crowne . . . [8]

Like the costumes displayed, the pattern of the procession in the chronicle play was fashioned after contemporary models. In addition, actual stage representation of recent spectacles pleasantly recalled events which colored the memories of many playgoers. At the celebration of the coronation of James I, an old man reported that he was witnessing his fifth such procession, indeed a reminder of the recurrence of these festivities in the Sixteenth Century. Henry VIII's coronation parade was followed by those of his wives, then by Edward's, Mary's and her husband Philip's, and finally by Elizabeth's. As the motion pictures today will exploit a successful device by repetition, so the Elizabethan dramatists found a constant public appeal in the staging of outstanding coronation processions of the Sixteenth Century.

Shakespeare and Fletcher recognized this appeal when they subtitled their *Henry VIII*, "All is True." Thus audiences were attracted to the Globe by the prospect of viewing exact reproductions of such spectacles as the procession to the trial of Katherine, the parade returning from the baptism of Elizabeth, and most magnificent of them all, the coronation procession of Anne Boleyn, for which elaborate stage directions were set forth:

THE ORDER OF THE CORONATION

1. A lively flourish of trumpets.
2. Then two Judges.
3. Lord Chancellor, with purse and mace before him.
4. Choristers singing.   Music.
5. Mayor of London, bearing the mace. Then Garter, in his coat of arms, and on his head he wore a gilt copper crown.
6. Marquess Dorset, bearing a sceptre of gold, on his head a demi-coronal of gold. With him the Earl of Surrey, bearing the rod of silver with the dove, crowned with an earl's coronet. Collars of Esses.
7. Duke of Suffolk, in his robe of estate, his coronet on his head, bearing a long white wand, as High Steward. With him the Duke of Norfolk, with the rod of marshalship, a coronet on his head. Collars of Esses.
8. A canopy borne by four of the Cinque Ports; under it, the Queen in her robe, in her hair, richly adorned with

pearl, crowned. On each side her the Bishops of London and Winchester.

9. The old Duchess of Norfolk, in a coronal of gold, wrought with flowers, bearing the Queen's train.

10. Certain Ladies or Countesses, with plain circlets of gold without flowers.

Exeunt, first passing over the stage in order and state, and then a great flourish of trumpets.

IV, i, 36 s.d.

Like modern parades, this procession had its commentators, three gentlemen spectators who identified the participants, first by reading a list and then more directly:

2. GENT. A royal train, believe me. These I know. Who's that that bears the sceptre?

1. GENT.   Marquess Dorset;
And that the Earl of Surrey with the rod.
IV, i, 37 ff.

Off-stage features of the event are described—the crowds, "pageants and sights of honour," and the coronation ceremony itself. With regard to costumes, properties, and order of the participants, the stage direction reveals that "all is true" indeed in this procession which rather closely follows the source passage from Hall as quoted by Holinshed. Minor changes are made to facilitate the audience's recognition of the characters in the procession. In the chronicle, the Earl of Arundel carries the rod with the dove and Lord William Howard bears the rod of marshalship. In the play, these respective functions are assigned to the Earl of Surrey and the Duke of Norfolk, who appear earlier in the drama.

"All is True" overreached its mark with at least one member of the audience. Sir Henry Wotton, who was impressed by, yet critical of, the splendid processions wrote his nephew:

The King's players had a new play, called *All is True*, representing some principal pieces of the reign of Henry VIII, which was set forth with many extraordinary circumstances of pomp and majesty, even to the matting of the stage; the Knights of the Order with their Georges and garters, the Guards with their embroidered coats, and the like: sufficient in truth within a while to make greatness very familiar, if not ridiculous.[9]

High points of *The Famous History of Sir Thomas Wyatt,* by Dekker and Webster, were the coronation of Henry's daughter Mary and the royal entry of Philip into London. Thus the title page of the quarto advertises the play, "with the coronation of Queen Mary and the coming in of King Philip." However, the ceremonies are not to be found in this quarto, but in Part 1 of Thomas Heywood's *If You Know Not Me You Know Nobody,* which concerns "the troubles of Queen Elizabeth" before her sovereignty. Two coronation processions decorate this play. Mary's in Scene ii, is similar to, though less splendid than Elizabeth's, with which the play closes. When Philip makes his royal entry in this same play, he inquires about the absence of the favorably-reputed Princess Elizabeth from his reception. The welcoming ceremony itself includes a declaration of the united titles of the two rulers and establishment of the date for the wedding. The greatest scene of display was withheld from the spectacle lovers until the close of the play, when Elizabeth's triumphal coronation procession was staged. This event, vividly described in contemporary pamphlets and chronicles, had undoubtedly been recounted to or experienced by many in the audience. Heywood's stage direction calls for a procession of more than twenty people, including the Queen under the canopy which was a standard feature of stage and actual ceremonies. She is preceded by four trumpeters, the sergeant trumpeter with the mace, a purse bearer, Sussex with the crown, Howard with the sceptre, the Constable with the cap of maintenance, Chandos with the sword, and Thame with the collar and a

George. Then come "foure Gentlemen bearing the Canapy ouer the *Queene,* two Gentle-women bearing vp her trayne, six gentle-men Pensioners." After a march "about the stage in order," they are met by the Lord Mayor who presents Elizabeth with a purse and Bible, and announces that:

> A thowsand of your faithfull Cittizens
> In Veluet Coats and Chaines well mounted, stay
> To greet their royall Soueraigne on the way.[10]

After graciously thanking him, Elizabeth kisses the Bible, as she does in the contemporary report of the actual event.

Earlier in the play, Heywood's treatment of Philip of Spain not as a villain but as a kindly intervener for Elizabeth, understandably differs greatly from the attitude of Robert Wilson, whose *Three Lords and Three Ladies of London* was produced about 1589. Here, their entry a threat as well as a challenge to the honor of London, the Spanish Lords vie with the Londoners in the pomp and ceremony of public display.

Like the description of the Field of the Cloth of Gold in *Henry VIII,*[11] Wilson's depiction reflects the keen competition between England and other countries in the splendor of their ceremonies. Printed accounts of the receptions of foreign sovereigns, or of English nobility or ambassadors abroad reported the magnificence of entries on the continent and at the same time furnished ideas for local celebrations. The eager interest with which the English received these accounts of foreign pomp resembles that which present-day Americans display toward English royal ceremonies, and is evidenced by such pamphlets as that published in 1594 detailing the coronation of Henry IV of France. Likewise, William Segar reported the details of the King's royal entry into Rouen and his investment with the Garter in 1596. Appealing to this public interest in foreign ceremonies, Marlowe's *Massacre at Paris* stages the coronation procession of a French king. Henry III, who has succeeded to the throne, is welcomed to France on his return from Poland, and entering with his train, is greeted by cries of "viue le Roy." He orders celebrations by "barriers, tourny, tylte, and like disportes."[12]

Although the promise of a glittering parade drew many to the playhouse, the royal entry processions were used on stage for their dramatic as well as their pictorial effect. One feature of the actual entry which playwrights were quick to exploit concerned the tension and expectancy which always precede the entrance of a spectacle. To heighten the audience's anticipation, the display might be delayed by a speech or a short scene. Sometimes, to withhold the splendor and increase the audience's pleasurable expectation, an announcer of the procession would appear and deliver a speech, as in *Coriolanus,* where a Herald precedes the triumphal parade to proclaim Marcius' deeds to the spectators.[13] This technique is expanded in 2 *Henry IV* where, "longing for what it has not," expectation is increased by the breathless dialogue of the rush-strewers who excitedly perform their last-minute duties before "trumpets sound and the King and his Train pass over the stage."[14]

Even longer is the scene of anticipation preceding the military parade in *All's Well that Ends Well.* The widow and her daughter, with Violenta, Mariana, and "other Citizens" are watching for the troops. When they hear a tucket, the widow decides "they are gone a contrary way. Hark! you may know by their trumpets," and the spectators begin to disperse. After Helena's entry, "a march afar" is heard. "Hark you! they come this way," cries the widow. As Bertram enters with Parolles, leading a parade of "the whole Army," members of the procession are identified by the spectators (as is done in *Henry VIII.*) The disguised Helena strikes a poignant note as she pretends not to know her husband Bertram, and asks, "Which is the Frenchman?"[15]

Before the Duke's entry in *Measure for Measure* there is a series of antecedent short scenes which heighten the expectancy of the audience. In the first of these scenes, Angelo gives orders for the reception of the Duke who has sent a notification of his sudden return and a request to be met at the city gates, where he is to receive petitions against injustice. In the following scene, the absent Duke gives Friar Peter letters to re-deliver to him, and calls for trumpets to be brought to the gate. Tension mounts in the third scene, which reveals Friar Peter announcing that the trumpets have sounded twice and that "the generous and gravest citizens" are gathered as the Duke nears the gates.[16] The Duke has laid his plans, Angelo has assured himself that Isabella dare not speak, Friar Peter has found Isabella a location in the crowd from which she can approach the Duke, and anticipation is at its peak when the royal entry takes place. Another artistic device adds to the effectiveness of this climactic scene in *Measure for Measure*. As in the source play, *Promos and Cassandra*, the dramatic suspense of the situation is intensified by being placed within the contrasting frame of a ceremonious entry.

A dramatic climax occurring in a scene of stately and splendid entry is also to be found in *When You See Me You Know Me*, probably produced in the same year (1604) as *Measure for Measure*. The more extended ceremonies in Rowley's play encompass an outstanding entry and a famous fall. The Emperor Charles on his entrance to London is first met by Cardinal Wolsey, the Mayor and Gentlemen, and then by another splendid procession accompanying the Prince, who is preceded by a herald bearing the Collar and Garter, and attended by the guard and lords. After the Prince presents the Collar and Garter, trumpets sound, and the King's coming is announced. The carefully-arranged procession appears:

Enter the Heralds first, then the Trumpets, next the guard, then Mace bearer and Swords; then the Cardinall, then Brandon, then the King, after him the Queene, Lady Mary, and Ladies attending.

As formalities are exchanged, suddenly the Emperor complains of Wolsey's defiance of him in the French King's cause. Appropriately enough, Wolsey—whose ambition and love of worldly pomp have betrayed him—is swiftly accused and discharged in the midst of display and ceremony.[17]

On the other hand, in 2 *Henry IV*, Shakespeare accentuates not the extensive ceremonies of royal entry and welcome, but rather the tense situation itself, which he places within the formal frame of the royal procession. In Act V, King Henry V enters, at the head of his train. Probably he is returning from the coronation ceremonies at Westminster and wears his crown. "Now sits Expectation in the air" indeed, as the orderly procession approaches the ill-assorted group surrounding Falstaff. Hailed by the fat and leering knight with whom he earlier burlesqued the pomp and ceremony which now surround him,[18] Henry rebukes and dismisses the old man, and the procession sweeps on. This effective technique of placing an irregular incident within a framework of formality is at least as old as *Agamemmnon*, where the ceremonies of the hero's return and welcome are abruptly checked. A more recent favorite among the melodramatic devices is the disruption of a wedding, a ceremony which reaches its tensest moment in real life with an invitation to interruption: "let him speak now . . . "

As the Elizabethan play developed, the procession took on another dramatic aspect. In the form of the triumph, it became a conventional method for depicting a victorious hero at the height of his fortune. A favorite study of Elizabethans,

Roman history was filled with references to triumphal marches in which the victor was seated in a chariot, accompanied by a parade of his army and captives, and a display of his trophies. It is not surprising, then, that the victory over the Armada was celebrated by an Elizabethan version of the classical triumph. Elizabeth rode in a "chariot-throne" with four pillars supporting the canopy, which was topped by an imperial crown. Upon two lower pillars there were mounted figures of a lion and a dragon supporting the arms of England. The Queen's attendants included the French Ambassador, the Earl of Essex, the Privy Council and Nobility, the Judges of the realm, Ladies of Honor and Guards. The waits were stationed at Temple Bar where Elizabeth was presented with a jewel and received and welcomed to her "City and Chamber" by the Lord Mayor and his aldermen attired in scarlet.

Likewise heroes of Renaissance Italy and France were being honored with adaptations of classical triumphs, which also were reproduced at festivals and allegorized in literature.[19] Not only from their Latin histories, then, might Elizabethans learn of the Roman triumphs, but from paintings and descriptions of their revival on the continent. English playwrights found the triumphal entry especially useful for depicting a *hybris*-ridden king or general at the peak of his fortune. As in the "triumphs of Fortune," to be discussed below, such glory proves transient; later in the play the hero is alone and in disgrace.

The well-known phrase "and ride in triumph through Persepolis" set the keynote for the popular victory parade, both staged and described in *Tamburlaine*. The word "triumph" in the Persepolis passage refers to the classical conception of an elaborate procession in which the conqueror's chariot, frequently drawn by exotic animals, is followed and preceded by prisoners and the victorious army. This was the established pattern for the triumphal march of a proud king

or conqueror in dramas following *Tamburlaine,* which itself had such precedents as the dumb show in *Jocasta* where
Ambition's chariot is drawn by kings. But just as "the clas-
sics" by the time of Elizabeth had assimilated many varying
influences, these Roman triumphs had been transformed,
especially by Medieval allegory and Renaissance renditions
of the mythology of Greece and Rome. Earlier in sixteenth
century England, chariots of such classical deities as Mercury,
Venus and Cupid had been represented in pageant and masque, while these media had been influenced in turn by the
allegorical triumphs of medieval literature as expressed by
Dante and Petrarch.

In 1 *Tamburlaine,* in their flyting before the battle, Tamburlaine and the Emperor of the Turks, Bajazeth, both boast
of their future triumphal marches. Tamburlaine threatens to
have the attendants of his horses lead Bajazeth captive, while
the Emperor retaliates by vowing that the triumphal chariot of
his queen will be drawn by his opponent's captains. After
Bajazeth is captured, he is caged and made a "perpetual triumph" by Tamburlaine, according to the practice of the
Romans in displaying their noble prisoners.

Evidently contributing to the popularity of the play, the
exotic features of the triumph in Part I are exploited in
Part II, wherein occurs an entry as famous as that described
in the Persepolis passage:

Tamburlaine drawen in his chariot by Trebizon and Soria
with bittes in their mouthes, reines in his left hand, in his
right hand a whip, with which he scourgeth them. Techel-
les, Theridamas, Vsumcasane, Amyras, Celebinus: Natolia,
and Ierusalem led by with fiue or six common souldiers.

IV, iii, s.d.

Although he uses the triumphal procession to stress the height
of Tamburlaine's glory, Marlowe does not employ the sub-

sequently popular device which implies a moral by depicting first a triumphant, and then a fallen hero. As a matter of fact, even at the end of Part II, although Tamburlaine is dying, he places his son in the chariot as his successor. Thus Marlowe seems more interested in the symbolical and splendid aspects of the triumph in relation to the character of Tamburlaine. However, there is a moral implication of the unsteady fortunes of the great, reflected not in Tamburlaine's fate, but in that of his victims. This is especially true in the case of Bajazeth, who is depicted first in glory, boasting and confident of victory, and later in disgrace, dying as an exhibit in Tamburlaine's triumph.

The same pattern is used by Robert Greene and Thomas Lodge in *A Looking Glass for London and England,* where the triumphal entry of Rasni the conqueror is contrasted with a later depiction of a humble Rasni "in sackcloath." The play opens with a colorful procession as the victorious Rasni returns from the wars to be welcomed by his son, his sister, and the wife of the King of Paphlagonia. As part of the celebration, a pageant device is brought on stage: "a globe seated in a ship."[20] The fall which follows pride receives striking visual representation when, toward the end of the play, a sorrowful and suffering Rasni enters, meanly dressed, humble, and repentant.

The best examples of contrast between the triumphal entry and the fall are to be found in dramas dealing with Roman history and reflecting from the classical writers the association of the hero's triumph with his later death. Thus, these plays graphically dramatize a theme popular with classical and Elizabethan writers alike, the fickleness of the goddess Fortune, who brings a man to the summit of earthly triumph, only to cast him down to death or disgrace. A classical favorite in Renaissance England, Horace in his "Ode to Fortune," addresses her as one who will both upraise poor mortals of low degree, and

> Proud triumphs change
> To funeral trains.[21]

Seneca, especially Seneca in Elizabethan rendition, expresses the same theme. The play of "Agamemmnon" in *Seneca his Tenne Tragedies* contains the following speech of Euribates "added to the Tragedy by the Translator:"

> Loe here how fickle fortune gives but brytle fading joy.
> Loe, hee who late a Conquerour tryumphed over Troy,
>
> .   .   .   .
>
> And they that of his victory and comming home were glad,
> To sudayne mourning chaunge their myrth with heavinesse bestad.
> The lusty pompe of royall courte is deade:[22]

This dual strain of triumph and death received visual representation in the triumphal and memorial arches which, long after the death of a hero, stood as testimony to the triumphs in his life. Through the ages, such an arch was an impressive symbol, rich in significance. To some, it manifested the Stoic mutability-of-Fortune theme, as expressed by Horace and Seneca: the hero who had once marched in triumph now lay in the dust. To others, the arch represented a testimony of fame: it offered material assurance that the memory of the great persisted in the world which they had left. By a further extension, which reversed the original triumph-to-death concept, still others found in the arch the implication of the spiritual triumph of the hero over death. While underlying actual Renaissance triumphs, these moral and philosophical associations become more clearly defined in the action and imagery of the drama.

Thomas Lodge's *The Wounds of Civil War* was one of the

earliest of the classical history plays to emphasize the pride-
to-fall theme by juxtaposing the triumph and the funeral. The
two most outstanding stage effects concern these events in the
life of the Roman leader Sylla. His elaborate victory march
highlights Act III:

Enter Scilla in triumph, in his car triumphant of gold,
drawn by four Moors; before the chariot, his colours, his
crest, his captains, his prisoners . . . bearing crowns of gold,
and manacled. After the chariot, his soldiers' bands: Basillus,
Lucretius, Lucullus besides prisoners of divers nations, and
sundry disguises.

III, i

A contrasting ceremonial closes the play "in great pomp," with
the funeral of Sylla,

> the man that made the world to stoop
> And fetter'd fortune in the chains of power

who now

> Must droop and draw the chariot of fate
> Along the darksome banks of Acheron.

V, i

In his dramas based upon Roman history—*Titus Andronicus, Coriolanus,* and *Julius Caesar*—Shakespeare presents a
similar pattern. A triumphal entry early in the play is balanced against a later funeral or fall from fortune. The opening of *Titus Andronicus* is ceremonious. In a series of mannered processions the Tribunes and Senators enter, to take
their places "aloft," and Saturninus and Bassianus appear "at
opposite doors" with their followers, and go into the Senate
house. Anticipation is aroused as a captain announces the coming of Titus:

> Romans, make way. The good Andronicus,
> Patron of virtue, Rome's best champion,
> Successful in the battles that he fights,

With honour and with fortune is return'd
From where he circumscribed with his sword
And brought to yoke the enemies of Rome.

> I, i, 64 ff.

The visual appeal of the opening scene reaches a climax as the triumphal procession enters: (See Plate II).

Sound drums and trumpets; and then enter two of Titus' sons, and then two men bearing a coffin covered with black; then two other sons; then Titus Andronicus; and then Tamora, the Queen of Goths, and her two sons, Chiron and Demetrius, with Aaron the Moor and others, as many as can be.

> I, i, 69 s. d.

In keeping with Roman custom, the victorious Andronicus is "bound with laurel boughs." The almost-obligatory association of the funeral and triumph, implicit in the entry itself, occurs when Marcus in his welcoming oration addresses the following Senecan sentiments to Titus' dead son in the coffin, "you that sleep in fame:"

> But safer triumph is this funeral pomp
> That hath aspir'd to Solon's happiness
> And triumphs over chance in honour's bed.
> I, i, 176 ff.

Perhaps, like Tamburlaine and Sylla, Titus entered in a chariot, for he mentions this necessary property later in the ceremonies:

> And here in sight of Rome, to Saturnine,
> King and commander of our commonweal,
> The wide world's Emperor, do I consecrate
> My sword, my chariot, and my prisoners.
> I, i, 246 ff.

After his entry in triumph, Titus' actions prompt Tamora's warning against *hybris*: "Wilt thou draw near the nature of the gods?" As the scene draws to a close, he remains on a stage which the others have deserted for the wedding and queries, "Titus, when wert thou wont to walk alone?"[23] Thus Shakespeare effectively compresses pride and fall within a single scene. *Tamburlaine* was concerned entirely with its hero's triumphs. *The Wounds of Civil War* balanced victory and disaster. After a brief but vivid display of the triumph, *Titus Andronicus* depicts the unfolding calamities of the fall.

Coriolanus follows the same formula of contrast between the hero's spectacular and crowded triumphal entry and his later fall and loneliness. There is the customary preparation for the splendid entry. A small group of spectators mirrors the audience's anticipation; the trumpets blast, and a Herald announces that Marcius returns from his victory over Corioli. The procession appears, proceeds about half-way across or around the stage, and halts while Coriolanus is welcomed by his mother, his wife, and Valeria.[24] A conventional device, the "stopped procession" increased the tension and prolonged the spectacle.

In Act IV, in a manner most foreign to the pomp of his entry, Coriolanus departs from Rome alone. Though the old Cominius offers to accompany him, the hero refuses the offer, in consideration for his friend's age, and requests that Cominius "Bring me but out at gate."[25] Here, Shakespeare may have been working consciously to effect a contrast between Coriolanus' solitary departure and his victorious entry, since in North's Plutarch, the banished hero is accompanied by "three or foure of his friendes . . . "[26] Cominius juxtaposes triumph and death in his description of the terrible destruction of Corioli by Marcius.[27]

In *Julius Caesar*, Shakespeare varies the customary pattern (as seen in *Titus Andronicus* and *Coriolanus*) of a glorious victory contrasted with a subsequent disaster. The many allusions to Julius Caesar in triumph reveal that the Elizabethans considered the name of this conqueror as practically synonymous with "triumphal march." In actual royal entry celebrations in the Renaissance, Caesar figured prominently, often represented in the pageants as a member of the Nine Worthies of history or alluded to in the speeches by way of flattering comparison to the personage welcomed. For instance, Henry VII was to be welcomed to Worcester by a Janitor, asking if the celebrated entrant was Noah or Jason,

> Or is it Julius with the Triumphe of Victorie
> To whom I say welcome most hertely.[28]

In *The Three Lords and Three Ladies of London,* Nemo announces that festivities will celebrate the wedding of the three couples who will proceed to church for the ceremonies, and

> With greater ioy wil they returne anone
> Than Caesar did in Rome his Laurell weare.[29]

So exalted by love is Gaveston in Marlowe's *Edward II,* that, he asserts,

> . . . I thinke my selfe as great
> As Caesar riding in the Romaine streete,
> With captiue kings at his triumphant Carre.
> ll. 172 ff.

A more appropriate association is found in a dramatic scene at the end of the anonymous *Edward III,* where Salisbury reports to the King that Prince Edward is losing the battle. Then there is a flourish, and a herald enters to announce Edward's victory and the approach of his triumphant procession. Upon his entry, Edward presents the "wreath of conquest" (King John's crown) to his father, fulfilling Audley's prophecy that the Prince would gain "A Caesars fame in kings captiuitie."[30]

In scenes concerning royal processions, Shakespeare frequently alludes to the triumphal marches of the famous Ro-

man. When the funeral procession of Henry V enters at the beginning of 1 *Henry VI,* the Duke of Bedford in a short elegy
laments the King's death, invokes his ghost to preserve peace
in the realm, and apotheosizes the dead Henry as follows:

> A far more glorious star thy soul will make
> Than Julius Caesar . . .

> I, i, 55 f.

At his entry to London in *Richard III,* the young Prince pays
tribute to the triumph of Caesar's fame over his death, since
he "lives in fame though not in life."[31] Later in the play,
Richard, in suing for the hand of Elizabeth, boldly compares
himself to the triumphing Caesar:

> Bound with triumphant garlands will I come
> And lead thy daughter to a conqueror's bed;
> To whom I will retail my conquest won,
> And she shall be sole victoress, Caesar's Caesar.

> IV, iv, 333 ff.

An allusion to Caesar provides a humorous contrast in *Measure for Measure* when Lucio, spying the ragged procession of
Elbow and his seedy officers leading the disconsolate Pompey
to jail for venery, addresses the prisoner with mock respect,
"How now, noble Pompey? What, at the wheels of Caesar? Art
thou led in triumph?"[32]

With Julius Caesar already established as the representative Roman triumpher, the audience at Shakespeare's play
about this hero would have been far from disappointed with
the opening scene presenting a gathering of townspeople to
await Caesar's triumphal entry. However, even to the least
alert, it was soon evident that the triumph was tarnished, for
it celebrated a victory not in a foreign war, which would be
sanctioned by Shakespeare's countrymen, but in a civil war,
dreaded by a people who still recalled the lesson of the Wars
of the Roses. Before Caesar's entry, the tribunes explicitly

remind the fickle celebrators that this is a "triumph over Pompey's blood"[33]—the sons of the former Roman hero. When the victorious Caesar finally appears with his train, Shakespeare does not emphasize his hero's valor but rather his superstition, for Caesar is seen anxiously instructing Antony to touch Calphurnia in the course of his race and cure her barrenness. By dismissing the soothsayer, Caesar reveals his affliction with that flaw peculiar to the great—*hybris*.[34] Criticism of Caesar's victory parade following a civil war is brought out in North's translation of Plutarch, where it is recorded that

... the triumph he made into Rome for the same, did as much offend the Romaines and more, then anything that euer he had done before: because he had not ouercome Captaines that were strangers, nor barbarous kings, but had destroyed the sonnes of the noblest man in Rome ... [35]

Quite in the classical tradition, Caesar's funeral recalls his triumph. The sight of Caesar's body after his murder in the Senate prompts Antony to make the inevitable association, as he laments:

> O mighty Caesar! dost thou lie so low?
> Are all thy conquests, glories, triumphs, spoils,
> Shrunk to this little measure?
>
> III, i, 148 ff.

There is a juxtaposition of visual effects as well. Yet the humble funeral procession, in which Antony is the only mourner following the coffin, is something more than a vivid contrast to the entry at the opening of the play. Subtly conceived by Shakespeare, the triumph, wherein glamor surfaced evil, had foreshadowed the fate which was to follow.

Shakespeare and his fellow playwrights achieved additional dramatic effects by manipulation of the procession. Sometimes, it was more effective to understate the elaboration expected.

For example, in *Alexander and Campaspe,* John Lyly avoids the triumphal entry usually associated with his hero. Almost equalling Caesar's popularity among the Elizabethans, the conqueror Alexander the Great was a standard member of the Nine Worthies of history, the representation of which became a favorite subject for pageants. As in the case of Julius Caesar, the mention or exhibition of Alexander the Great was invariably in connection with a triumph. In the dumb show after the first act in *The Scottish History of James IV,* for instance, Alexander enters in great pomp to behold the tomb of Cyrus. And Labesha, in Chapman's *An Humorous Day's Mirth,* finds it necessary to correct an amateur show which has erroneously considered Fortune and not Alexander the conqueror of the world. As a member of the Nine Worthies Show in *Love's Labour's Lost,* Alexander stands forth and announces:

When in the world I liv'd, I was the world's commander—
V, ii, 565

It might be expected then, that *Alexander and Campaspe* would open with the splendor of a triumphal march as Alexander returned victorious from battle. However, like those who applauded the Restoration heroic plays, the members of Lyly's audience in the private theatre cared less for triumphal marches or stage skirmishes than they did for the sentiments of a hero stricken by love which deters him from his duty. Accordingly, Lyly's play begins quietly, with the entrance of Timoclea, Campaspe, and other prisoners of the conqueror. Then Alexander appears and dismisses the captive ladies with a promise that they shall be "honourably entreated," and "all wants . . . supplyed." "In conqueste milde, as beseemeth of a King,"[36] Alexander is as unlike Tamburlaine—the favorite of the popular stage—in his entry as he is in character. Lyly does not emphasize the conqueror's military splendor, but rather his mildness, his love soliloquies, and his final conquest of love by duty.

Even playwrights of the popular stage might forego the splendor of a royal entry in favor of a more dramatic effect. In *The Fair Maid of Bristow,* as in *Henry V,* the king's return from victory in a foreign land is the occasion for a celebration. In the former play, King Richard arrives from the Holy Land to be welcomed at Bristol with the announcement of a forthcoming "tryumphe." The King replies that he would willingly celebrate,

> But for this unlucky accident
> Which makes old Eustice and Vmphreuil sad . . . [37]

Here the promise of splendor is unfulfilled, as the situation is darkened by the seriousness of the plot.

A similar device is effectively employed by Shakespeare in *Richard III.* In the probably earlier *True Tragedy of Richard III,* as well as in Holinshed's account, Richard and Buckingham meet the young King at Stony Stratford to accompany him to the city, and the new sovereign's entry to London is not depicted. Holinshed reports that the mayor rode out with his men to meet the new King at Hornsey. In the *True Tragedy* the small train which accompanies the Prince to London is accounted for by his mother's reminder that the town of Northampton was unable to provide for an extensive retinue (a situation which Elizabeth had often to reckon with when arranging her progresses.) In addition, it is decided that a large group of followers might be construed as evidence of the Prince's malice against Gloucester and his blood. In Shakespeare's play, however, at the general court conference, it is the Machiavel Buckingham who suggests the small train as an insurance of good-will among the nobles. Ironically enough, the proposal is approved by Rivers who is later arrested *en route.*[38]

The facts of entry portrayed in *Richard III* deviate from the sources. Into one scene at the gates of London, Shakespeare compresses the Prince's arrival, his welcome by his enemies Richard and Buckingham, and his reception by the Mayor. Here at the gates, usually decorated with pageants and surrounded by cheering citizens on such occasions, stands the Prince with his "little train." Buckingham utters a one-line welcome, followed by Richard's ironical advice regarding the discrepancy between men's hearts and tongues.[39] By introducing the spectacle, Richard evades the Prince's persistent questions about his arrested uncles, and announces the arrival of the aldermen and the Lord Mayor (soon to support Richard for King). Here, as in his imagery, Shakespeare achieves an artistic contrast between the somberness of the particular entry he depicts and the joy which is usually associated with such occasions. The later plans for coronation pomp[40] only emphasize the meagreness of the entry ceremonies and intensify the foreboding regarding the Prince's end in the Tower. This edifice, of course, was the customary departure point of the coronation procession to Westminster.

Shakespeare again employs the "muted entry" in *Richard II*. While the ruler's appearance in public was customarily surrounded with pomp and ceremony, here a dethroned King enters, under guard, on his way "to Julius Caesar's ill-erected tower."[41] The Queen, who has been awaiting his arrival, cries out:

> Ah, thou the model where old Troy did stand,
> Thou map of honour, thou King Richard's tomb,
> And not King Richard! Thou most beauteous inn,
> Why should hard-favour'd grief be lodg'd in thee
> When triumph is become an alehouse guest?
> > V, i, ll ff.

To the Queen, Richard's person, like the popular pageant figure of an honored sovereign, is representative of the true king, "the model where old Troy did stand." She mourns that grief should be housed in so fair a form while triumph inhabits the less noble person of Bolingbroke. Richard's lament at the end of the scene recalls the pride-to-fall pattern. His Queen, who had entered England with such ceremony,

> . . . set forth in pomp,
> She came adorned hither like sweet May,

must return in disgrace,

> Sent back like Hallowmas or short'st of day.
>
> V, i, 78 ff.

The situation, a gloomy one at best, is further darkened by such reminders of customary pomp as the Tower, Julius Caesar, the triumph of Bolingbroke, and the Queen's former entry. Immediately following, and in direct contrast to the parting of Richard and his Queen, comes the Duke of York's description of the parade of the victorious Bolingbroke, "Mounted upon a hot and fiery steed," amidst the cheers and blessings of the people.[42]

Shakespeare seldom if ever describes or stages an entry which is not suggested in his source. However, he realizes not only the visual but the dramatic value of the procession, for tension in *Measure for Measure, All's Well that Ends Well,* and 2 *Henry IV;* for the depiction of proud characters—Titus Andronicus, Coriolanus and Julius Caesar—who later fall from Fortune; and for effective contrasts of actual somberness with customary joy in *Richard III* and *Richard II.*

PROCESSIONS DESCRIBED

WHILE many debatable points in Shakespeare's works have furnished food for theses, critics have unanimously agreed in praising his vivid descriptions. In this respect, perhaps some measure of consideration should be given to the audience who wanted to *see* as much as possible of what transpired, whether it was a spectacular entry or a gory murder. If limitations prevented the physical depiction of an event, the audience was unsatisfied with colorless reporting. Descriptive passages might evoke an emotion or create a mood, but they had primarily to paint pictures for the mind's eye to behold. In the drama, the concreteness and color of passages describing entries can be attributed in part to the destination, but also to the source, the popular reports of these events in chronicles, pamphlets, poems, and ballads.

Abundant descriptions of the pomp of royal ceremonies in such chronicles as Hall's recreated the spectacle for the reader, and also advertised to the world the magnificence and power of the Tudors. For example, Anne Boleyn's coronation procession, staged in *Henry VIII*, is fully detailed in Hall's chronicle, which especially celebrated the Tudors. The accounts found in Hall are reprinted by Holinshed, omitting some of the descriptive detail, but retaining enough to provide the reader with pictures of the splendor of the sixteenth century sovereigns. Earlier royal ceremonies were outlined in the histories of Froissart and Fabyan. These chronicle accounts of royal entries influenced both the staged processions and the descriptive passages; the latter sometimes reflected the style and approach of the history sources, which stressed the procession itself and the size of the crowd, and offered editorial comment on the main participants in the parade.

The description of the entry of Henry IV into London in *Richard II* resembles the technique of the chronicles. A carefully sketched picture contrasts two characters and stresses the large and enthusiastic crowd whose support is so important to the new King. The passage is related by the Duke of York, who recounts to his wife the entry into London:

> Then, as I said, the Duke, great Bolingbroke,
> Mounted upon a hot and fiery steed
> Which his aspiring rider seem'd to know,
> With slow but stately pace kept on his course,
> Whilst all tongues cried 'God save thee, Bolingbroke!'
> You would have thought the very windows spake,
> So many greedy looks of young and old
> Through casements darted their desiring eyes
> Upon his visage; and that all the walls
> With painted imagery had said at once
> 'Jesu preserve thee! Welcome, Bolingbroke!'
> Whilst he, from the one side to the other turning,
> Bareheaded, lower than his proud steed's neck,
> Bespake them thus, 'I thank you, countrymen.'
>
> V, ii, 7 ff.

Like the chronicler, the narrator of the passage often editorialized upon the scene he described. Here York serves as a chorus character, expressing his own pity for Richard, and thus establishing the pattern for the audience's response:

> . . . men's eyes
> Did scowl on gentle Richard. No man cried
>   'God save him!'
> No joyful tongue gave him his welcome home,
> But dust was thrown upon his sacred head;
> Which with such gentle sorrow he shook off,
> His face still combating with tears and smiles
> (The badges of his grief and patience),
> That, had not God for some strong purpose steel'd
> The hearts of men, they must perforce have melted
> And barbarism itself have pitied him.
>
> V, ii, 27 ff.

Just as many modern newspaper readers seek full reports of current ceremonies, so were the Elizabethans receptive to printed accounts of recent entries, progress entertainments, or Lord Mayor's Shows. Such pamphlets gave some details about the royal procession and the crowd, and described at

length the settings, costumes, and import of the pageants.
The speeches were reported in full, as were the devices which
had been prepared but not presented because of the whim of
the weather or the prince. This fetish for including every
detail of the entertainments would point to the author of
the shows as the one who customarily prepared the pamphlet. Overly proud pageanteers had their critics among the
playwrights. In Ben Jonson's *The Case is Altered,* Antonio
Balladino, "Pageant Poet to the City," makes a characteristic inquiry as to whether his latest display was witnessed by
Onion, whom he had just met. Onion answers "No faith sir,
but their goes a huge report on't," to which Antonio replies
expansively . . . "I'll giue you one of the bookes, O you'le like
it admirably."[43]

It is impossible to tell how many of the Elizabethan readers who sought the colorful descriptions in the pamphlets
realized their advertising aim. The same is true, of course, of
the spectacles themselves, from the days of the Roman triumphs
to the present. Certainly it was advantageous for a guild to
print accounts of its Lord Mayor's Shows and for a nobleman
to publish a quarto detailing the devices with which Elizabeth had been entertained on his estate. Likewise it was
profitable to the sovereign and to the subjects when their
mutual love was stressed by these reports.

Characteristically, the printed account of a public ceremony extravagantly praised the personage honored, and frequently compared him to a famous figure in history or legend.
The pamphlet describing Queen Elizabeth's coronation eulo-
gizes the nonpareil Queen and celebrates the mutual love of
ruler and subject in the following manner:

So that if a man shoulde say well, he could not better tearme
the Citie of London that time, than a stage wherein was shewed
the wonderfull spectacle, of a noble hearted Princesse toward
her most loving People, and the People's exceding comfort

in beholding so worthy a Soveraigne, and hearing so Prince like a voice, which could not but have set the enemie on fyre, since the vertue is in the enemie always commended, much more could not but enflame her naturall, obedient, and most loving People, whose weale leaneth onely uppon her Grace and her Government.[44]

Equally fulsome were the praises of James in pamphlets and poems celebrating his entry. Some of these favorably compared James to Augustus Caesar, the bringer of peace.

Reminiscent of the pamphlet reports is the description in *Henry V* of that conqueror's triumphant entry to England after Agincourt. Here Shakespeare details the wild enthusiasm of the people, and likens the nonpareil ruler to an appropriate worthy:

> But now behold
> In the quick forge and working house of thought,
> How London doth pour out her citizens!
> The Mayor and all his brethren in best sort—
> Like to the senators of th' antique Rome,
> With the plebeians swarming at their heels—
> Go forth and fetch their conqu'ring Caesar in;
>
> V, Ch. 22 ff.

While Shakespeare comfortably compares the London burghers to antique Romans, Marlowe's imagination is fired by the exotic elements of the classical triumphs. This splendor he describes with all the detail characteristic of the printed accounts. In 2 *Tamburlaine,* such a triumph is promised to his keeper by Callapine, as an incentive to release him:

> With naked Negros shall thy coach be drawen,
> And as thou rid'st in triumph through the streets,
> The pauement vnderneath thy chariot wheels
> With Turky Carpets shall be couered:
> And cloath of Arras hung about the walles,
> Fit obiects for thy princely eie to pierce.
> A hundred Bassoes, cloath'd in crimson silk,

Shall ride before the on Barbarian Steeds:
                    I, iii, 2531 ff.

Thus, with the magnificence of the Renaissance royal entry, Marlowe enriches the Roman conception of the triumph— the chariot of the victor, the captured trophies, chained prisoners and marching army. He further decorates his descriptions with mythological characters and personified abstractions from the pageants and the allegorical "triumph literature," to be discussed below. In the Third Act of Part II, Theridamus pictures Tamburlaine as a hero

> That treadeth Fortune vnderneath his feete,
> And makes the mighty God of armes his slaue:
> On whom death and the fatall sisters waite
> With naked swords and scarlet liueries:
> Before whom (mounted on a Lions backe)
> Rhamnusia beares a helmet ful of blood,
> And strowes the way with braines of slaughtered men:
> By whose proud side the vgly furies run,
> Harkening when he shall bid them plague the
>   world.
> Ouer whose Zenith, cloth'd in windy aire,
> And Eagles wings ioin'd to her feathered breast,
> Fame houereth, sounding of her golden Trumpe:
>   III, iv, 3463 ff.

Here in the formal tableau grouping of the pageant, the gods of war and fate attend on the victory chariot of Tamburlaine, who has triumphed over Death and Fortune to be favored by Fame.

The descriptions of triumphs in *Tamburlaine* reflect not only the ostentation with which the English chroniclers were concerned, but also the effect on the pride of the victor and the humiliation of the captor, as stressed by the classical histories. Using elements of the magnificent entry, Marlowe's hero envisions his triumphal march through his native Samarcanda after he has conquered all the world:

Thorow the streets with troops of conquered kings,
Ile ride in golden armour like the Sun,
And in my helme a triple plume shal spring,
Spangled with Diamonds dancing in the aire,
To note me Emperour of the three fold world,

.   .   .   .

Then in my coach, like Saturnes royal son,
Mounted his shining chariot, gilt with fire,
And drawen with princely Eagles through the path,
Pau'd with bright Christall and enchac'd with starres,
When all the Gods stand gazing at his pomp.
So will I ride through Samarcanda streets,
Vntil my soule disseuered from this flesh,
Shall mount the milk-white way and meet him there.

Pt. 2, IV, iii, 4093 ff.

In the classical tradition of the proud triumpher, Tamburlaine here "draws near the nature of the gods." He compares himself to Apollo, who was frequently associated with the triumphs because of the splendor of his own course across the sky in a gold chariot. In similar passages, a warning to the triumpher against pride might be contained in an allusion to Apollo's son, Phaeton, who aspired to equal his father's glorious ride and was destroyed.

The anonymous *Caesar and Pompey* of c. 1605 likewise demonstrates the *hybris* of the hero by a comparison between the triumphing Caesar and the god of the sun:

The Tyrant mounted in his goulden chayre,
Rides drawne with milke white palferies in like
   pride,
As Phoebus from his Orientall gate,
Mounted vpon the firy Phlegetons backes.

III, i

Whereas Marlowe admired Tamburlaine for his boldness, in *Caesar and Pompey* the *hybris* is recognized as a flaw, as it is in the classical models. A disintegration of character is marked by Caesar's daring "to match ould Saturns Kingly sonne," and calling:

> Cassiopea leaue thy starry chayre,
> And on my Sun-bright Chariot wheels attend,
> Which in triumphing pompe doth Caesar beare.
>
> III, ii

While the classical histories praised the victor, with due warning against *hybris,* they represented being led in triumph as unbearable shame for a vanquished hero. This attitude is reflected in *Antony and Cleopatra,* where the very mention of the word "triumph" shakes the thoughts of the splendor-loving Queen of Egypt and her noble Roman paramour. In the final test, they prefer death to the supreme disgrace of decorating Caesar's triumph. In the case of Antony, his Roman pride revolts against the humiliation which defeat would bring. To spur Eros to kill him, the general demonstrates the subservience to which he would be brought as a chained follower of Caesar's triumphal chariot:

> She, Eros, has
> Pack'd cards with Caesar and false-play'd my glory
> Unto an enemy's triumph.
> . . . .
> Wouldst thou be window'd in great Rome and see
> Thy master thus with pleach'd arms, bending down
> His corrigible neck, his face subdu'd
> To penetrative shame, whilst the wheel'd seat
> Of fortunate Caesar, drawn before him, branded
> His baseness that ensu'd?
>
> IV, xiv, 18 ff; 72 ff.

Antony cruelly pictures a similar fate for Cleopatra as he upbraids her for her desertion in battle:

> Vanish, or I shall give thee thy deserving
> And blemish Caesar's triumph. Let him take thee
> And hoist thee up to the shouting plebeians.

> Follow his chariot, like the greatest spot
> Of all thy sex. Most monster-like be shown
> For poor'st diminitives, for doits . . .
>
> IV, xii, 32 ff.

While the Roman general cannot bend his glory to the degradation of being led in triumph, the Egyptian Queen is not so fearful of reputation as she is filled with revulsion at the proximity of the "shouting plebians," between whose thick breaths and herself, in her most famous public appearance, there intervened a river.[45] Obsessed with the offensive picture of being exhibited in Caesar's victory march, she even refuses to descend to the dying Antony,

> Lest I be taken. Not th' imperious show
> Of the full-fortun'd Caesar ever shall
> Be brooch'd with me!
>
> IV, xv, 23 ff.

On the other hand, Caesar is most anxious to display Cleopatra in his triumphal procession. Believing that her presence in Rome would constitute an eternal triumph, Octavius sends Dolabella to guard her life, in accordance with the motive ascribed by Plutarch: "He thought that if he could take Cleopatra and bring her aliue to Rome, she would maruellously beautifie and set out his triumphe.[46] In answer to her question, Dolabella assures Cleopatra of Caesar's intent to lead her in triumph, and thus strengthens her resolve to kill herself, after a final thought of the crowds to which she would be exhibited:

>   Mechanic slaves,
> With greasy aprons, rules, and hammers, shall
> Uplift us to the view. In their thick breaths,
> Rank of gross diet, shall we be enclouded,
> And forc'd to drink their vapour.
>
> V, ii, 209 ff.

SOVEREIGN AND SPECTATOR

A "MECHANIC" in Shakespeare's audience would not require an acquaintance with Aristotle to realize that Cleopatra's attitude toward the crowd is, like many of her other actions, unqueenly. But this groundling might console himself with the thought that Cleopatra, an Egyptian, represented the bad example of a public-appearing ruler. Indeed, like most other media, the drama took its turn at playing courtesy book, and exhibited for those who list heed the ideal behavior for sovereign and spectator upon public occasions. Such events were, of course, more than a source of visual enjoyment. They were a matter of political importance to the ruler and of civic and national pride to the citizens, many of whom had contributed their own services or money to the display.

The glory of a royal entry in London not only impressed the onlookers with the splendor of the sovereign, but also advertised to other countries the wealth and might of England. It is to be expected that the drama would reflect this important function as well as the technical aspects of public celebrations. Pomp, one of the Lords in *The Three Lords and Three Ladies of London,* is praised by his page Wealth, who points out that "Pomp" means "magnificence" and represents the "sumptuous estate without pride or vaineglorie."[47] Thus "Magnificence" in Elizabethan times, besides signifying sumptuousness or splendor, also retained some of its Aristotelian meaning of "liberal expenditure in good taste." When the Spanish challenge is received, Policie instructs Pomp and Pleasure as to their competition with Spain in the important matter of magnificence:

> Lord Pomp, let nothing that's magnificall,
> Or that may tend to Londons graceful state
> Be unperfourm'd, As showes and solemne feastes,
> Watches in armour, triumphes, Cresset-lightes,

Bonefiers, belles, and peales of ordinance.
And pleasure, see that plaies be published,
Mai-games and maskes, with mirth and minstrelsie,
Pageants and school-feastes, beares, and puppit
    plaies . . .

Pomp agrees to let the visitors know "Honor in England, not in Spaine doth grow."[48]

The occurrence and extent of such pomp was, of course, to be regulated. Concerned with the private and public virtues of the ruler, the Elizabethans felt that the degree of formality and frequency with which the sovereign exhibited himself in public should be neither exceeded nor minimized. Chronicle writers and playwrights of the period diplomatically found the perfect example in the practices of their Queen.

Advising his son in this regard, Henry IV warns against such a model as the "skipping King" Richard, who appeared in public so often and so informally as to surfeit the public of his sight. Rather, Henry recommends that the sovereign's display of himself to the public be "seldom but sumptuous."[49] The wisdom of this advice is borne out in York's above-quoted description of the entry into London where Bolingbroke holds the public's attention, while Richard is carelessly regarded. Likewise criticized is the lavishness, especially in private entertainments, of "idle triumphes, maskes, lasciuious showes," of which Edward II is accused in Marlowe's play.[50] And Shakespeare's King John is reminded by his court advisors that his insisting on repeated coronation ceremonies is painting the lily.[51]

The appearance of a sovereign in public with a lack of proper ceremony is equally deplored. In *Caesar and Pompey*, Pompey is distressed that his humble entry into Egypt is so inappropriate to his station, and laments:

I was not wont to walke thus all alone,

> But to be met with troopes of Horse and Men.
> With playes and pageants to be entertayned,
> A courtly trayne in royall rich aray
>
> .   .   .   .
>
> Mounted on steeds, with braue Caparisons deckt,
> That in their gates did seeme to scorne the Earth.
> Was wont my intertaynment beautiefie.
>
> II, iv

Shakespeare too is aware of the proper standards of "magnificence" in the public appearances of royalty. Not to be found in Plutarch, but more likely in Shakespeare's own experience of Elizabeth's progresses is this model which the angry Octavius contrasts with his sister's unpretentious trip to Rome in *Antony and Cleopatra*:

> The wife of Antony
> Should have an army for an usher, and
> The neighs of horse to tell of her approach
> Long ere she did appear. The trees by th' way
> Should have borne men, and expectation fainted,
> Longing for what it had not. Nay, the dust
> Should have ascended to the roof of heaven,
> Rais'd by your populous troops. But you are come
> A market-maid to Rome, and have prevented
> The ostentation of our love, which, left unshown,
> Is often left unlov'd. We should have met you
> By sea and land, supplying every stage
> With an augmented greeting.
>
> III, vi, 43 ff.

The crowds along the road, the clouds of dust raised by the procession, the "augmented greeting" at every stage of the journey—all were customary features of Queen Elizabeth's trips about England on summer progress.

The arrival of Florizel and Perdita in *The Winter's Tale*, without the ostentation expected of visiting princes, of course arouses Leontes' suspicion:

> He comes not
> Like to his father's greatness. His approach,
> So out of circumstance and sudden, tells us
> 'Tis not a visitation fram'd, but forc'd
> By need and accident. What train?
>
> V, i, 88 ff.

The ideal sovereign's duty upon public occasions only began with striking the proper balance as to both frequency and ostentation. There was more to be displayed than magnificence. As energetically stressed by the pamphlet accounts, the ideal ruler exhibited his love and concern for his people who in turn (ideally) cheered him with shouts demonstrating the loyalty which was in their hearts. Following the practice of the pamphlets, poems, and chronicles, the staged and described entries in the drama took into account this important relationship between the crown and the crowd.

The entries which Shakespeare stages are witnessed by a few actors who serve as spectators and commentators and represent the attendant crowd. These groups of three to five persons include Falstaff and his crew in 2 *Henry IV;* the widow, her daughter, friends, and Helena in *All's Well that Ends Well;* Virgilia and Valeria (with Brutus and Sicinius aside) at Coriolanus' entry; and the three gentlemen in *Henry VIII.* Just as the chronicles and pamphlets detailing a public spectacle always included a depiction of the vast crowds, so were these throngs reported in the drama, whether the entry itself was described, or staged before a small group of witnesses. Descriptions of the attendant multitudes are found in *Richard II, Henry V, Julius Caesar, Coriolanus,* and *Henry VIII;* the crowds are at least suggested in *Measure for Measure.*

All of Shakespeare's accounts of the crowd have some features in common. First, they include an over-all picture of the throng, a perpendicular effect of "living walls" of people.

For example, in the Duke of York's description of Boling-broke's entry in *Richard II,* men, women and children fill up all the window space of the houses which wall the streets:

> You would have thought the very windows spake,
> So many greedy looks of young and old
> Through casements darted their desiring eyes
> Upon his visage; and that all the walls
> With painted imagery had said at once
> 'Jesu preserve thee! Welcome, Bolingbroke!'
>
> V, ii, 12ff.

Satisfying in its total effect and puzzling in its parts, this passage compresses a number of "flash impressions" which an observer would receive upon such an occasion. The windows crammed with people suggest a living wall, as mentioned. At the same time, in the same lines there are reflections of the pageant which was associated with the entry. Not too unlike the effect of people at building windows, actors were displayed, more artistically of course, in niches in the façade of the pageant. "The walls with painted imagery" may refer to the painted cloths hung from the house windows and depicting human figures labelled with the words they were supposed to be speaking.[52] Shakespeare's audience would recall too, the city walls, exhibiting upon their gates at these celebrations, pageants in which painted panels bore such common mottoes as "Jesus preserve thee" and "Welcome."

Observing the same obligation to describe the crowd at the entry of Henry IV, Samuel Daniel in his poem on the *Civil Wars* achieves quite a different effect:

> Where all, of all degrees, striue to appear;
> Where diuers-speaking Zeale one murmure findes . . .
>
> II, 63.

A typically Shakespearean description of crowds attendant upon a spectacle is the passage in *Julius Caesar* quoted at the beginning of this chapter, where the crowd awaiting Pompey fills windows and walls, towers, battlements, and even chimney tops. A similar impression of height is given in *Coriolanus* by Brutus' report of the throng waiting to greet the victorious Marcius:

> Stalls, bulks, windows
> Are smother'd up, leads fill'd, and ridges hors'd
> With variable complexions, all agreeing
> In earnestness to see him.
>
> II, i, 226 ff.

This description is reminiscent of Dekker's account of James' entry, reported at the beginning of this chapter.

Along with his visual image of the multitude as a "living wall," Shakespeare conveys an auditory appeal, as he refers to and reflects the sound of the people's cheers for their prince. When describing the ruler's first appearance upon the scene, Shakespeare effectively uses onomatopoeia to suggest by short, stressed words like "shout," "clap," and "roar," the spontaneous outburst of noise, followed by such longer words approximating the echoes and reechoes of the shouts, as "replication," and "salutation." For instance, Henry IV tells his son that his appearances before the people won him "Loud shouts and salutations from their mouths."[53] And in reminding the people of Pompey in *Julius Caesar,* the Tribune recalls that

> . . . when you saw his chariot but appear,
> Have you not made an universal shout,
> That Tiber trembled underneath her banks
> To hear the replication of your sounds
> Made in her concave shores?
>
> I, i, 48 ff.

At the shore to welcome the triumphantly returning Henry V are his subjects "whose shouts and claps outvoice the deep-

mouth'd sea."[54] The commons in *Coriolanus* make "a shower
and thunder with their caps and shouts," in celebration of
Marcius' triumph,[55] while Pistol in 2 *Henry IV* announces
the offstage shouts preceding the coronation entry of Henry
V, with "There roar'd the sea."[56]

Besides special effects of sight and sound, a third distinc-
tive feature of Shakespeare's descriptions of crowds welcoming a royal entry is his individualizing of some of the members of the multitude. Sometimes the picture is an unpleasant
one; Cleopatra shudders at the thought of the "mechanic
slaves" with their greasy aprons, who would throng to see her
in Caesar's victory march. With them may be compared the
good-natured but shallow-minded artisans whom Marullus
berates at the beginning of *Julius Caesar* because they re-
spond to any spectacle, regardless of the worth of the man
whom they celebrate. However, just as the Duke of York expresses pity for Richard II in the entry of Bolingbroke, so
might the passages in *Antony and Cleopatra* and *Julius
Caesar* be colored not necessarily with Shakespeare's strictures,
but those of his speaker. Marullus' disparagement of the fickle
multitude is prompted by his own sensitivity and patriotism.
While perhaps reflecting King James' own aversion to the
mob,[57] Cleopatra's contempt for crowds is appropriate to her
own abhorrence of the physically offensive, as opposed to her
luxuriousness and indulgence of the senses. Richard II, always playing to an audience, conceals his envy of Bolingbroke's popularity with a supercilious sneer at the craftsmen,
draymen and oyster wenches who have thronged to greet the
Duke and wish him well on his journey.[58] Himself "ambi-
tious for poor knaves' caps and legs"[59] the tribune Brutus,
his comments touched with both scorn and wonder, describes
the people who make up the crowds at Coriolanus' entry:

> Your prattling nurse
> Into a rapture lets her baby cry

> While she chats him. The kitchen Malkin pins
> Her richest lockram 'bout her reechy neck,
> Clamb'ring the walls to eye him.
>
> > II, i, 222 ff.

A messenger reports further:

> I have seen the dumb men throng to see him and
> The blind to hear him speak. Matrons flung gloves,
> Ladies and maids their scarfs and handkerchers,
> Upon him as he pass'd; the nobles bended
> As to Jove's statue, and the commons made
> A shower and thunder with their caps and shouts.
> I never saw the like.
>
> > II, i, 278 ff.

As in Brutus' description, different types of persons are pictured forgetting their customary pursuits to do homage to a hero.

Attributed to Fletcher, the description of the crowd attendant upon the coronation of Anne in *Henry VIII* includes many of the conventional items: the noise, the size of the throng, the waving of caps. However, the passage does not convey the effect of "living walls," characteristic of Shakespeare, nor does it individualize members of the group by their occupations and properties. Also missing is the onomatopoeia, although there is employed a favorite Shakespearean comparison between the sound of the crowd and that of the sea:

> . . . such a noise arose
> As the shrouds make at sea in a stiff tempest,
> As loud, and to as many tunes. Hats, cloaks
> (Doublets, I think) flew up; and had their faces
> Been loose, this day they had been lost. Such joy
> I never saw before. Great-bellied women
> That had not half a week to go, like rams
> In the old time of war, would shake the press

> And make 'em reel before 'em. No man living
> Could say 'This is my wife' there, all were woven
> So strangely in one piece.
>> IV, i, 71 ff.

The final scene of *Henry VIII*, also ascribed to Fletcher, presents a novel departure from Shakespeare's method of suggesting offstage crowds by a small group of representative spectators on stage. Instead, cries offstage and the lively action of two actors who try to hold off the invisible horde convey the impression of a vast and unruly throng. As the procession from the baptismal service of the Princess Elizabeth is expected to arrive, the porter and his man attempt to curb the pushing, enthusiastic multitude awaiting the entry. The size and disorder of the crowd are suggested by the offstage shouts and by the remarks of the porter and his assistant, who jest over their rough treatment of this mass of people whom the helper suggests be swept back, whiffler fashion, with cannons:

> 'Tis as much impossible,
> Unless we sweep 'em from the door with cannons,
> To scatter 'em as 'tis to make 'em sleep
> On May Day morning, which will never be.
>> V, iv, 12 ff.

Blamed for admitting the mob to the courtyard, the Porter's man replies:

> I am not Samson, nor Sir Guy, nor Colebrand,
> To mow 'em down before me;
>> V, iv, 22 f.

implying that only one of these popular pageant giants might effectively clear a path for the oncoming parade. Finally the Lord Chamberlain enters to announce the arrival of the procession, and to send the porter and his helper out as whifflers to prepare the way:

> Go break among the press and find a way out
> To let the troop pass fairly, or I'll find
> A Marshalsea shall hold ye play these two months.

PORT. Make way there for the Princess!
MAN.   You great fellow,
> Stand close up, or I'll make your head ache!
PORT. You i' th' chamblet,
> Get up o' th' rail. I'll peck you o'er the pales else!
>   V, iv, 88 ff.

In staging and describing the popular processions, Shakespeare and his fellow dramatists reflect more than the stylistic trends of their printed sources and the technical aspects of the actual occasions. The plays also reveal the prevailing Elizabethan attitude regarding public appearances of the ruler and his relationship to his subjects at these events.

*   *   *

In the lives of the average Elizabethan citizen, the scenes of spectacle were provided by the royal processions. In the popular playhouses, the same procedure was followed, with the same enthusiastic reception. While printed accounts supplemented the real-life pageants and processions, the playwrights added verbal to visual magnificence by describing those entries or parts of entries which were not staged. But staging and relating the splendors of the entry on the Elizabethan stage aimed at more than visual nourishment. The procession was a striking symbol. Moral implications of the transience of pomp and earthly glory were expressed by the juxtaposition of a victory march and a funeral, or by the presentation of a triumphing hero who later was cast down by Fortune. In exploring the dramatic possibilities of the stage procession, playwrights found that short preceding scenes of expectation and excitement aroused the anticipation of the audience and increased the pleasurable impression of the entry. They discovered too the effectiveness of employing the formal procession as a contrasting frame for dramatic climax. Lastly, the Elizabethan current of opinion was reflected in plays which revealed the civic and national importance of proper royal ceremony and suggested the standards of behavior on such occasions for sovereign and spectator.

CHAPTER TWO

The Royal Reception

ORATIONS

IN THE tranquil days before the invention of electrical public address systems, the effect of the spoken word was lost upon many of those who thronged to the royal celebrations. This factor discouraged neither the extent nor the energy of the official welcoming oration, but it did mean that much of the impression to be made depended upon the visual effect. Thus, besides the elaborate displays, in the public ceremonies themselves gesture was broad and stylized and movements symbolic. At a royal entry the ceremonies of welcome began after the sovereign and the splendid procession had entered the main gate of the city. First, a formal oration was delivered by a representative of the city—the Mayor, the Recorder, or, on occasion, a schoolmaster. Then the city magistrates would render up such symbols of their offices as the mace and the staff to the sovereign, who re-conferred these tokens. Next, the ruler was presented with a substantial gift, generally money in a "standing cup" or purse. In addition, the key to the city was sometimes bestowed upon her, according to a practice which has persisted.

Long, formal and Ciceronian, the welcoming address ex-

emplified the Elizabethans' interest in and practice of the
classical oration. The form was familiar to most schoolboys
of Shakespeare's day, when the curricula included the study
and imitation of rhetoric.[1] Undoubtedly required reading
for successful city and court officials, handbooks such as Wilson's *Arte of Rhetorique* gave advice on the preparation and
delivery of this important and intricate form. The address
made by Recorder Edward Aglionby at Warwick in 1572 is
a representative welcoming oration. Following the prescrip-
tions as outlined in Wilson's book, Aglionby began by stating
the occasion for his speech, which was "in the manner and custom . . . begonne by the Greeks, confirmed by the Romaynes
. . . called panegyrics." He continued with an *apologia* for
his lack of skill, a narration of the history of Warwick and a
catalogue of the favors received from sovereigns, including
honors bestowed by Elizabeth, who created Ambrose Dudley
Earl of Warwick. The speech concluded with an expression
of the joy of the townspeople and assurance to the Queen of
their dutiful hearts. The presentation of the gift followed.
Not infrequently, the oration was in Latin, as was the case at
Norwich in 1578 where the Mayor eulogized the Queen and
affirmed the devotion of her subjects, with a wish "that the
bright beame of your most chast eye, which doth so chere us,
might penetrate the secret strait corners of our hartes." Then
came the rendering of the signs of office and bestowal of the
gift.[2] This speech followed Wilson's model for "an oration
in praise of a man," where it was advised that the orator de-
scant upon the worthiness of the honored personage, and
give events "before his life," (i.e., his genealogy), and "in
his life," that is, his "education, inclination of nature as
skills and attempts worthie."[3]

Would-be public speakers might also have consulted Puttenham's *The Arte of English Poesie* for instruction "In what
forme of Poesie the great Princes and dominators of the world

were honored." For such eulogies, Puttenham recommended the mention of dead princes as examples to those living, "shewing their high estates, their Princely genealogies and pedegrees, marriages, aliances, and such noble exploites, as they had done in th' affaires of peace and of warre to the benefit of their people and countries . . . "[4]

Generally, the ruler's remarks upon such occasions were limited to brief expressions of gratitude. Testimony to the fact that the sovereign sometimes delivered orations at public celebrations is to be found in *The Merchant of Venice,* when Bassanio tells Portia:

> . . . there is such confusion in my powers
> As, after some oration fairly spoke
> By a beloved prince, there doth appear
> Among the buzzing pleased multitude,
> Where every something, being blent together,
> Turns to a wild of nothing, save of joy,
> Express'd and not express'd.
>
> **III, ii, 177 ff.**

With regard to her speeches, Queen Elizabeth seems to have had a perfect sense of timing and occasion. Brief remarks and gracious gestures were for the multitude. Formal orations in Latin or Greek impressed the scholars at Oxford and Cambridge.

In addition to the welcoming addresses at the universities, the "entertainment" consisted of debates, in which the speeches followed classical models. The formidable length of these orations is revealed by an incident which occurred during the Queen's visit to Oxford in 1592. Anthony Wood reports in his *Annals* that at this time the Bishop's oration in the debate on "whether it be lawful to dissemble in cause of religion" was so extensive that the Queen sent twice to him to instruct him to shorten it, because she wished to make a public address herself that evening. As the Bishop's speech continued

to grow, the Queen's patience diminished, and she finally can-
celled her own oration.

The scene of the Emperor's visit to Oxford in Robert
Greene's *Friar Bacon and Friar Bungay* follows the pattern
of the actual progresses of Elizabeth to the seats of learning.
On his entrance to the school, the Emperor delivers a eulogy
of Oxford, which is followed by a debate more visually appealing than the ones Elizabeth had witnessed at the same
school two years before Greene's play was published. In *Friar
Bacon and Friar Bungay,* the dispute concerns the relative importance of spirits of pyromancy and geomancy in magic. After each magician-scholar argues his case, Vandermast for pyromancy and Friar Bungay for geomancy, the *confirmatio* is
presented in the form of a show which concerns a favorite
subject of the pageants—the labors of Hercules.[5] Bungay's
conjuration produces the tree with the golden apples of the
Hesperides, complete with a dragon shooting fire. Vandermast then produces Hercules himself, attired in a lion's skin.
The German's confutation of Bungay's skill is successful, for
Hercules, in accordance with the legend, begins to break the
branches of Bungay's golden tree. Just as defeat seems certain for the English magician, Bacon appears, and confutes
both Vandermast and the legend. Although he has the Emperor order a disputation between Bacon and the German
scholar, Greene apparently realized that the point of maxi-
mum interest had been reached in the debating scene, which
finishes with a flourish as Hercules, at Bacon's command,
carries off Vandermast and the tree.

Published in the same year as *Friar Bacon and Friar Bungay,* Thomas Nashe's *The Unfortunate Traveler* probably
says the last satiric word on the university receptions. Jack
Wilton reaches the University of Wittenberg just in time to
witness the arrival of the Duke of Saxony, whom the orator
of the university welcomes with an address

al by patch and by peece meale stolne out of Tully . . . but to show the extraordinarie good will they bare the Duke, (to have him stand in the raine tyll he was thorough wet) a thousand *quemadmodums* and *quapropters* he came over him with, every sentence he concluded with *Esse posse videatur*: through all the nine worthies he ran with praising and comparing him, Nestor's yeares hee assured him off under the broade seale of their supplications, and with that crowetrodden verse in Virgil, 'Dum juga montis aper,' hee packt up his pipes and cride *dixi*. [6]

Thomas Nashe was not alone in recognizing the humorous aspects of the highly artificial, complex and obligatory welcoming oration. While Nashe satirized the tired rhetoric and incredible exaggeration, dramatists found inherent in the ceremonious welcome one of the bases of comedy—incongruity. Irresistibly amusing was the aspect of a group of burghers attempting the characteristic bombast of the welcoming speech. The occasion all too frequently brought out the pretentious among the pedants and *illiterati* alike, both fair game for comic representation upon the stage.

In Anthony Munday's *John a Kent and John a Cumber*, Turnop, "my Lordes man" contends with the Sexton, who claims to hold "an office of retoritie," for the privilege of delivering the welcoming oration to the noblemen:

Enter TURNOP *wth his crewe of Clownes,* & *a Minstrell.*

TURNOP: Nay neuer talke of it, Hugh the Sexten stutters, let him read the first lyne, or see if he can say the speeche, that dawes our Churchwarden made in prayse of his Mill horsse.

HUGH: It makes no matter, I think my selfe the wisest because I am Sexten, and being Sexten, I will say the speeche I made my selfe.

331 ff.

Turnop is finally chosen, and energetically displays the learning which has fitted him for the office of orator:

well, for your wisedomes, in chusing me, I rest quoniam dig
nitatis vestrum primarion, as the Poet Pediculus sayth, at the
next vestrie, bound to deferre ye to seuerall locall places.

. . . .

HUGH: Thats because he has a little more learning, an [d] has
borrowe[d] the vshers olde coat to grace him selfe withall.
351 ff.

At the ensuing welcome, Turnop's rhetoric is as extravagant
as it is confusing:

Like to the Cedar in the loftie Sea,
Or milke white mast vppon the humble mount:
So hearing that your honors came this way,
Of our rare wittes we came to giue account.
Ffor when as princes passe through pettie townes
They must be welcom'd, least they tearme vs clownes.
372 ff.

A similar dispute takes place in the anonymous *A Knack to
Know a Knave*, where the men of Gotham seek a properly
learned representative to address the entering King. Seriously
concerned with "How to misbehave our selues to the Kings
worship," the Miller nominates the Smith, "for hees a wise
man." A dissenting voice comes from the cobbler, who feels
that the Mayor is a more accomplished candidate: "Naigh-
bor, he shall not doe it, as long as Jefferay the Translater is
Maior of the towne."[7]

That "unfortunate traveller," Jack Wilton, experiences a
reception of the Duke by "the burgers and dunstical incorpora-
tioners of Wittenberg," in which a "bursten belly inkhorne
orator" most learnedly welcomes the visiting noble and presents the gift:

... Oratorie, uncaske the bard hutch of thy complements, and
with the triumphantest troupe in thy treasurie do trewage unto

·him. What impotent speech with his eight partes may not
specifie, this unestimable guift, holding his peace, shall as
it were (with teares I speake it) do whereby as it may seeme
or appear to manifest or declare, and yet it is, and yet it is
not, and yet it may bee a diminutive oblation meritorious
to your high pusillanimitie and indignity . . . . I here . . . .
offer up unto you the Cities generall good will, which is a
guilded Canne in manner and forme following, for you and
the heeres of your bodie lawfully begotten to drinke healths
in . . .[8]

Since learning, variously defined, was a prerequisite for
the welcoming oration, schoolmasters and scholars often figured in such occasions. They were called upon not only to
prepare orations, but also to deliver them before the Queen.
At the gates of the hospital in Norwich in 1578, the master
of the grammar school, Stephen Limbert, was to address the
Queen in Latin, extolling her mercy and charity to poor men
and her general benefits to all her subjects. But his nervous-
ness was noticed by the Queen who "drewe neare unto him,
and thinking him fearefull, saide graciously unto him: Be
not afrayde.' " He then proceeded "with good courage." After
the oration, Elizabeth praised Master Limbert, gave him her
hand to kiss, and departed for the court, but "sente backe
to know his name."[9]

This "publike Scholemaster" is evidently the "Mr. Lam-
bert" whose farewell oration to the Queen was preserved,
but not presented because time was lacking. With the ub-
iquitous alliteration which characterized the form, he was to
extoll as an example of "the force of friendshippe and fam-
iliarity," Theseus, whose faithfulness was "commended by
the mouth and monumentes of all men" whom nothing could
"sequester from their sweete society and comfortable company."[10] Interestingly enough, Theseus in *A Midsummer
Night's Dream* demonstrates this behavior for which Limbert
had praised him, and reflects Elizabeth's own customary

graciousness to the orators on such public occasions. As he is about to witness the entertainment proferred by Bottom and company, Theseus remarks to Hippolyta:

> Where I have come, great clerks have purposed
> To greet me with premeditated welcomes;
> Where I have seen them shiver and look pale,
> Make periods in the midst of sentences,
> Throttle their practis'd accent in their fears,
> And, in conclusion, dumbly have broke off,
> Not paying me a welcome. Trust me, sweet,
> Out of this silence yet I pick'd a welcome;
> And in the modesty of fearful duty
> I read as much as from the rattling tongue
> Of saucy and audacious eloquence.

> V, i, 93 ff.

Suggestive of speeches which were prepared by scholars are the lines in 2 *Return from Parnassus*, where the student Academico reminds Amoretto, "My name is Academico Sir, one that made an oration for you once on the Queenes day, and a show that you got some credit by."[11] Academico's claim to have written a show for the royal celebration reveals that the schoolmaster often contributed more than the oration. For the welcoming show at Kenilworth, for instance, Richard Mulcaster, the headmaster of St. Paul's, wrote the verses which accompanied the gifts of the gods. Since children usually were the actors and sometimes even the orators at royal receptions, a natural choice for writer and director of the shows was the schoolmaster, who, like Parson Evans in *The Merry Wives of Windsor* when the fairy dance is planned, "will teach the children their behaviours."[12] Similarly, it is schoolmaster Holofernes whose assistance Don Armado seeks in *Love's Labour's Lost* when he has been asked by the King to arrange a show for the visiting Princess. It was perhaps inevitable that friction develop between the professional writers hired by the cities or the nobles to devise entertainments for the Queen on progress, and these local scholars. Reflecting the bitterness between poet and pedant, Thomas Churchyard reported of the shows at Bristol in 1574, "Some of these speeches could not be spoken, by means of a Scholemaister, who envied that any stranger should set forth these Shows."[13]

In the character of Rombus, Sidney's "Lady of May," a progress entertainment at Wanstead in 1578, satirized the pretentious schoolmaster and the pedantry he inflicted upon these shows. Rombus stepped forward as the prologue to a contest which was to be played between foresters and shepherds, "and with many special graces, made this learned Oration." With Latin flourishes, he introduced himself and continued, "Wel, wel *ad propositos revertebo;* the purite of the veritie is that certain *Pulcra puella profecto* . . . hath been *quodammodo* hunted, as you would say, pursued by two, a brace, a couple, a cast of young men, to whom the craftie coward *Cupid* had *inquam* delivered his dire-dolorous dart." When the Foresters and the Shepherds debated their respective merits after a singing match, Rombus interrupted to remind them to use the proper classical form: "Why you brute Nebulons, have you had my *Corpusculum* so long among you, and cannot yet tell how to edifie an argument? Attend. . . . First you must divisionate your point, etc."[14]

With similar comic incongruity, the schoolmaster in *The Two Noble Kinsmen* delivers an impressive, thirty-four-line exposition as introduction to the simple morris dance presented by the country people. With its forced rimes and galloping metre, his speech seems to parody those delivered at the entertainments. Such Churchyard-like alliteration as

> And, dainty Duke, whose doughty dismal fame
> From Dis to Daedalus, from post to pillar,
> Is blown abroad . . .
>
> III, v. 114 ff.

is reminiscent of Holofernes' epitaph on the "pretty pleasing pricket" in *Love's Labour's Lost*.[15]

A playwright staging a welcoming ceremony might give his audience comedy as well as spectacle, but he was more wary when it came to presenting the "learned oration" itself on the Elizabethan stage. The moving, colorful royal entry procession was an effect to be prolonged; on the other hand, the static welcoming oration which followed was, as a general rule, considerably condensed. The effect of the fuller oration can be seen in George Whetstone's *Promos and Cassandra*, published in 1578 and used by Shakespeare as the source for *Measure for Measure*. Although its visual effects, including an entry and pageant, suggest that it was written for stage presentation, *Promos and Cassandra* was never acted. It is interesting, however, not only as a source for a Shakespearean play, but also as an early example of the stage depiction of elements of the royal entry. In Part 2 of Whetstone's play, after delivering up his sword of office to the entering King, Promos makes "his briefe Oration." Following the pattern of a conventional Elizabethan welcoming address, he expresses the joy of the citizens at the arrival of the ruler, whom they assure of their good will and zeal:

> Reknowned King, lo here your faithful subiects preass to show
> The loyall duetie, which (in ryght) they to your highnesse owe.
> Your presence, cheares all sorts of vs: yet ten times more we ioye,
> You thinke vs ffoarde, our warning short, for to receyue a Roye.
> Our will, is such, as shall supplie, I trust in vs all want,
> And where good wyll the welcome geues, prouision syld is scant.
> Loe, this is all: yea, for us all, that I in wordes bestowe,
> Your Maiestie, our further zeale, in ready deedes shall knowe.   I, ix

By the time of Shakespeare, the playwrights had reduced such orations to one or two lines, had used them to further the dramatic action, or had turned them to serve humorous effects as noted above. A comparison may be made between the oration in *Promos and Cassandra* and the corresponding one in *Measure for Measure*. In Shakespeare's play, as pointed out, first the anticipation is heightened preceding the Duke's arrival, then the citizens gather at the gate, and finally the Duke appears. Angelo and Escalus speak one line of welcome to the entering ruler: "Happy return be to your royal Grace." And, instead of presenting a typical and static Elizabethan eulogy of the honored personage, Shakespeare achieves an effect of dramatic irony by having the Duke deliver a speech in praise of his welcomer Angelo, whose fame will triumph over time:

> O, your desert speaks loud, and I should wrong it
> To lock it in the wards of covert bosom
> When it deserves, with characters of brass,
> A forted residence 'gainst the tooth of time
> And razure of oblivion. Give me your hand,
> And let the subject see, to make them know
> Favours that keep within.
>   V, i, 9 ff.

The last lines carry the same implication as the closing of Promos' speech, which assures the King that the deeds of his subjects will prove their inner feelings of zeal.

In *Richard III*, the welcoming ceremony is similarly turned to dramatic effect. As successor to the throne, the Prince enters the city of London to be greeted by only a one-line welcome from Buckingham, whose aptness for oratory is expressed later to Richard,

> . . . I'll play the orator
> As if the golden fee for which I plead
> Were for myself.   III, v, 95 ff.

At the Prince's entry, Buckingham's terse "Welcome, sweet Prince, to London, to your chamber," may be an intentional reminder of the royal entries' customary pomp, in which the Prince's arrival is sadly lacking. Since the decorated London streets through which a sovereign passed on the way to the coronation claimed to be, in a special sense, the royal "chamber," Buckingham may be using the word with these implications.[16] The characteristically extensive speech of the Mayor is also cut to a single line, as Shakespeare employs abbreviated ceremonies, in addition to the straggling train, to accentuate the somberness of a customarily happy occasion.

In some cases, however, the long oration might be retained to intensify the suspense. In the entry scene in Rowley's *When You See Me You Know Me,* there are seventy-five lines of welcome and reply, broken by stage movement. The visiting Emperor Charles of Austria is greeted first by the Cardinal; then the Prince enters, makes a welcoming address, presents the collar and garter, and confers upon the Emperor the order of Knight of the Garter. After Henry VIII enters with his retinue, there are further lines of mutual eulogy before the accusation and dismissal of Wolsey.

Occasional speeches presented before the ruler in real life and in drama not only praised the prince, but also treated topical subjects, sometimes with a request for favor hinted or directly expressed. Welcoming Henry VII to York in 1486, Ebrancus diplomatically followed a catalog of the Ruler's virtues with an expression of hope for grace from the new King for the impoverished city. At Worcester, in 1575, the orator reminded Elizabeth of the favors of former sovereigns to the once-flourishing city in which now "wealth wasted and decayed." The cause, continued Mr. Bell, was to be found in "unlooked-for troubles, as the breach of faith lies in merchants, and restraint of trafyque . . . now restored by your maj-

esties Prynceley prudense . . ." Pirates upon the seas, he stated,
were another impediment to the prosperity of the city, which
hoped that the English navy would take action to "represse
those robberes."[17] Likewise the men of Gotham, whose "applauded Merrimentes . . . in receiuing the King into Goteham" were a feature advertised on the title page of *A Knack
to Know a Knave,* petition the entering King to allow them
to brew strong ale thrice a week and to enact a provision
that "he that comes to Goteham, and will not spende a penie
on a pot of Ale, if he be a drie, that he may fast,"[18] i.e., that
food will not be served unless accompanied by ale.

While they might have been condensed or turned to dramatic or comic effects, the orations in the drama recognizably
followed the established forms. Representative speeches honoring "the great Princes and dominators of the world" are
the encomium of Elizabeth at the end of Peele's *Arraignment of Paris,* and the complimentary addresses in the long
welcome in *When You See Me You Know Me.* It would seem
too that in the drama many a eulogy pronounced for a dead
hero followed the conventional patterns as they were prac-
ticed in real life. Cranmer's oration at the baptism of Elizabeth at the end of *Henry VIII* applies Puttenham's rules
for celebrating "the natiuitie of Princes children," by "prays-
ing the parentes by proofe, the child by hope, the whole kin-
dred by report, & the day itselfe with wishes of all good suc-
cesse, long life, health & prosperitie for euer to the new
borne."[19] Actually, the speech functions as a eulogy of the
dead Queen.

In actual and staged addresses of welcome there is a strongly recurrent figure which is not to be found in the instruction
books. To assure the sovereign of the people's love, the almost invariable image is one of loyal hearts as expressed by
truthful tongues. For instance, in Henry Petowe's verses on

James' entry the people

> Lift up their voyces; on their heart-strings play
> Crying, "Haile, Caesar!" with a shrill-toung'd streyne:[20]

This combination of true tongues and hearts which expresses the subjects' welcome, love and allegiance to the sovereign, is to be found again and again in pageant speeches and in scenes in plays where the sovereign enters a city or an estate. At Elizabeth's coronation, a child who delivered verses in Latin and English offered the Queen the blessing tongues and true hearts of her subjects. In the farewell address at Norwich, the Queen was told that the tongue was inadequate to "expresse our secrete joyes of hart,"[21] while at Cowdray in 1591 Elizabeth was given a gold key signifying that the owners' "tongue is the keie of his heart: and his heart the locke of his soule."[22] Welcomed and presented with a purse by the Mayor in 2 Promos and Cassandra, the King replies

> And for this time as outward showes make proofe,
> It is inough (and all that I desire)
> That your harts and tongues (alyke) byd me welcome.
>
> I, ix

The same theme is employed with dramatic irony in *Richard III* at the Prince's entry into London when the hypocritical Gloucester tells the boy that he lacks discernment in distinguishing between men's hearts and tongues:

> Sweet Prince, the untainted virtue of your years
> Hath not yet div'd into the world's deceit.
> No more can you distinguish of a man
> Than of his outward show; which, God he knows,
> Seldom or never jumpeth with the heart.
> Those uncles which you want were dangerous.
> Your Grace attended to their sug'red words
> But look'd not on the poison of their hearts:
>
> III, i, 7 ff.

In 1 *Henry IV*, the King confesses to his son a deliberate

"courtship to the common people" which succeeded, he says, in winning him the loyalty of their hearts as well as the praises of their tongues:

> ...I did pluck allegiance from men's hearts,
> Loud shouts and salutations from their mouth . . .
> III, ii, 52f.

While the ceremonies of greeting, the pageant themes, and even the speeches were growing more or less standardized, the image of loyal hearts and true tongues was becoming a characteristic feature of almost all welcoming orations, whether in real life or upon the stage.

SONGS AND SHOWS OF GREETING

JUST AS PLAYWRIGHTS recognized that the welcoming oration *per se* had little dramatic appeal, so the more entertainment-minded showmakers sought novel means of greeting the honored personage. Verses and songs early came into favor, to precede, follow, or in some instances supplant the reception speech. Sometimes, the welcomer was costumed as a character from the history or legend connected with the visited locale or with the visitor's life. In his 1486 progress, Henry VII was greeted at York by the figure of Ebrancus, the city's legendary founder, and when Elizabeth visited Norwich in 1578, there rode in the procession which met her "one which represented King Gurgunt, sometyme Kyng of Englande, which buylted the Castle of Norwich, called Blanch Flowre, and layde the foundation of the citie." As they neared the town, Gurgunt was to have come forth with a speech (prepared but not delivered because of rain) giving his identity and reminding Elizabeth of their common interests: each of them had an ancestor who united England after internal brawls; Gurgunt had founded, and Elizabeth had favored, Cambridge University.[23] Similarly, the plans for the celebration of James' entry called for the King to be met by actors attired as the Genius of the city of London, accompanied by St. George and St. Andrew, the patron saints of England and Scotland. They were to praise the union of the two kingdoms, and to bid the King to enter Troynouvant. However, like Gurgunt's speech, this show was not performed.

Another figure at royal receptions was related more to the orations' characteristic use of prophecy than to the history of the ruler or the locale. Cranmer's oration in *Henry VIII* employs all of the conventional praises of the Queen, but the speech, delivered at Elizabeth's baptism, is in the form of a prophecy. It contains a compliment to James as well, since Cranmer foresees that Elizabeth will be succeeded by an heir "As great in admiration as herself."[24] But a prophetic oration or greeting was more vivid when delivered by the character who had prophecied the future to Aeneas—the sybil. This figure of classical myth became a picturesque prophet in the early liturgical plays,[25] and later an appropriate and colful character to greet the sovereign and foretell a happy future. At Kenilworth in 1575, a sybil welcomed Elizabeth and predicted an increase of the already-manifold virtues of the Queen who would reign free from war and be hailed as a Prince of Peace. The sybil seems to have been employed in trio in Matthew Gwynne's welcoming show at Oxford in 1605. Here "tres quasi Sybllae" hailed King James I as a descendant of Banquo and prophesied a long and happy reign to the sovereign of the newly-united countries of Scotia, Anglia and Hibernia.[26] A parallel to this Oxford greeting has been found in the appearance of the three weird sisters who foretell the future to Macbeth and who "prophet-like" hail Banquo as "father to a line of kings."[27]

On the noblemen's estates which the Queen visited on her progresses to the country, the formal oration disappeared altogether, being quite inappropriate to the atmosphere of myth, music and enchantment. It was replaced by welcoming songs sung by nymphs and fairies, or by poems of greeting recited by such figures as the porter who welcomed the ruler and delivered the keys of the house at Cowdray in 1591.

Many of these welcoming lyrics are notable for their sweetness and simplicity. The following was written by Thomas Watson and sung at Elvetham by the Graces and Hours who greeted the Queen with "a sweete song of six parts, to this dittie:"

> With fragrant flowers we strew the way,
> And make this our chiefe holliday:
> For though this clime were blest of yore
> Yet was it never proud before.
>   O beauteous Quene of second Troy,
>   Accept of our unfained joy.
> Now th'ayre is sweeter than sweet balme,
> And Satyrs daunce about the palme:
> Now earth, with verdure newly dight
> Gives perfect signe of her delight.
>   O beauteous Quene of second Troy,
>   Accept of our unfained joy.
> Now birds record new harmonie
> And trees doe whistle melodie;
> Now everie thing that nature breeds
> Doth clad itselfe in pleasant weeds.
>   O beauteous Quene of second Troy,
>   Accept of our unfained joy.[28]

In a similar vein is the part song sung by a choir to welcome Queen Juno to the happy hill of Ida in *The Arraignment of Paris*.

The smaller audience and more ample space on the estates permitted the devisers of the progress entertainments to experiment with ingenious methods of greeting the ruler, until little dramatic sketches came to be written for the purpose of celebrating the arrival of the Queen. In 1602, at Harefield Place, the Queen alighted from her horse to find herself the subject of a dialogue between Place, in a parti-colored robe, and Time, who carried a stopped hour glass. Time contended that Place was too small and insignificant to receive the Queen. In reply, Place pointed out that he had received the sun, which the sovereign Elizabeth resembled. A diamond heart was then presented to the Queen, as a mirror of the true heart of the donor.

Since the Sovereign's part in these episodes was limited to her mere appearance upon the scene, the showmakers especially favored for their greeting a device found in the pastoral and romance, wherein a wild man is tamed through the influence of a pure and virtuous lady. The playlet, then, concerned an uncivilized character who was either unaware of the Queen's approach, or unappreciative of her endowments. Immediately upon Elizabeth's appearance, however, he underwent a change wrought by the very sight of her. At Kenilworth, for instance, at the outer gate a porter who had been raging about the upset in the household became gentle in the presence of the Queen, asked her forgiveness, and opened the gates. On the way to Bisham in 1592, "the Cornets sounding in the Woods, a Wilde Man came forth," but at the sight of Elizabeth, he informed the entrants, "my untamed thoughts waxe gentle, and I feele in myselfe civility. . . . Thus Vertue tameth fierceness; Beauty, madnesse. Your majestie on my knees will I followe, bearing this Club, not as a Savage, but to beate downe those that are."[29]

Thus a feature of the pastoral was employed dramatically by the progress entertainments, which assisted in passing on

Plate I. Procession of Queen Elizabeth, visit to Blackfriars, 1600.

Plate II. Drawing by Henry Peacham, 1595, illustrating the tableau in *Titus Andronicus*, I, i.

this device to the Elizabethan pastoral dramas. In *Mucedorus,* for instance, a "wildeman" is similarly tamed by the sight of a beautiful and virtuous maiden. The savage Bremo finds he cannot strike Amadine:

> I cannot weeld my weapons in my hand;
> Me thinkes I should not strik so faire a one:
> I thinke her beawtie hath bewitcht my force . . . [30]

The convention, of course, remained popular in the entertainments, reaching its most artistic treatment at the hands of Milton in *Comus,* where the lady's virtue was proof against a villain more sophisticated and dangerous than his leaf-clothed, raging prototypes.

WELCOME GIFTS

AFTER THE WILD man had been transformed at Bisham, Ceres appeared and bestowed upon Elizabeth her crown of wheat ears and a jewel. Such a presentation marked the climax of the welcoming ceremonies. The standard gift in the cities was money presented in a purse or "standing cup" like the one the Mayor gave Elizabeth at Norwich in 1578, "of silver, and guilt, with a cover; and in the cup one hundreth poundes in golde." In accepting this gift, Elizabeth pointed out that "Princes have no neede of money . . . "but that she would receive it as a token of the citizens' good will, since the greatest riches are the loyal hearts and true allegiance of the subjects. Then, "the cover of the cup lifted up," to ascertain that the good will token was intact, she carefully delivered it to one of her footmen, with the caution "Look to it, there is a hundreth pound."[31] In *Promos and Cassandra,* the entering King is presented with a purse by the Mayor, who performs a similar function in the last scene of 1 *If You Know Not Me.*

In the latter play, Elizabeth also is given a Bible, as she was at her actual coronation celebration.

At the progress entertainments, the obligatory gifts were more original. As demonstrated by the crown of wheat ears and jewel from Ceres at Bisham, symbolic or occasional gifts were accompanied by those of permanent value. Ingeniously wrought jewelry filled both of these requirements. The inventory of gifts given to the Queen by nobles whose estates she visited in the summer of 1574 includes among its items a crystal falcon, its head, tail, legs and breast of gold, garnished with rubies and emeralds; a jewel of rubies and diamonds with a phoenix and salamander of agate; a dolphin made of mother of pearl and gold, with a man upon its back, garnished with diamonds and rubies; an eagle of gold enamelled green, and a mermaid of gold, with a maid upon her back.[32]

Gifts from the classical gods was a favorite theme for the presentation. Entering Kenilworth, the Queen passed over a bridge twenty-seven feet wide by seventy feet long, decorated with gifts sent by the deities of mythology. The presents were placed upon seven pillars erected on each side of the bridge. On the first pair stood Sylvanus' present, birds in a cage. On the next, were two great silver bowls with fruit from Pomona; on the third, wheat, barley, oats and other grains from Ceres. The remaining pillars bore gifts of grapes and wine from Bacchus, a tray of fish from Neptune, implements of war from Mars, and musical instruments from Phoebus, all accompanied by Latin verses composed for the occasion by Richard Mulcaster. In *The Arraignment of Paris,* similar gifts are given by classical deities to Queen Juno, Venus, and Pallas, who go on progress to Diana's Bower. Here they are welcomed by the presentation of fruits from Pomona, a lamb from Pan, a faun from Faunus and an oaken bough from Sylvanus. At the entrance, as her welcome device, Flora has made flower images of the visitors.

Perhaps, as J. W. Cunliffe has suggested,[33] the masque in *The Tempest* involves such a customary presentation by mythological goddesses. When the play was presented at court as part of the celebration of the betrothal of Princess Elizabeth, it would have been entirely according to practice for Juno and Ceres to deliver an actual gift to the Princess, as implied in the lines

> And some donation freely to estate
> On the bless'd lovers.
> IV, i, 85 f.

A standard feature of progress entertainments, masques, and tournaments, the bestowal of gifts upon an honored person may very well stem from the old "mummeries." According to this custom, a group of costumed figures visited the sovereign and brought him presents. Stow reports that in 1377, a "mummerie" of one hundred and thirty citizens in costume rode in procession through London and called on the Prince who was to become Richard II. One of the mummers was arrayed as an emperor, one as a Pope, and twenty-four as cardinals. They saluted the Prince,

shewing by a paire of dice vpon the table their desire to play with the Prince, which they so handled, that the Prince did alwayes winne when hee cast them. Then the mummers set to the Prince three jewels, one after another, which were a boule of gold, a cup of gold, and a ring of gold, which the Prince wanne at three casts.[34]

As early as the beginning of the fifteenth century, the presentation of gifts was a special feature of royal entertainments. John Lydgate, for example, was the author of a mummerie in which Bacchus, Juno and Ceres sent to the sovereigns gifts of wine, wheat and oil, symbolizing Peace, Plenty and Gladness. Elaborating on this tradition was the dinner show Elizabeth witnessed in 1578 at Norwich, where a procession of gods and goddesses in pairs entered, marched about the room, presented gifts and verses, and then departed. The gifts included a riding wand of whale's fin presented by Jupiter, a purse from Juno, and a white dove from Venus.

Just as the writers of the progress entertainments developed playlets to celebrate Elizabeth's arrival, so they also devised shows solely to provide occasions for the presentation of gifts. An example of such a practice can be seen at Rycote in 1592 where an old ex-soldier met the Queen and assured her of his continuing service, although he could not offer her his horse, his armor, shield or sword, since these had been taken by his four sons who had gone out to seek their fortunes at arms. On Sunday, after encountering the Queen again in the garden, the old gentleman received in succession messengers from Ireland, Flanders and France, with letters from his sons, who professed their love and duty to the Queen and sent appropriate gifts, such as a dart of gold set with diamonds bearing a motto in Irish; a gold key adorned with diamonds, from Flanders; and from France, a sword of gold and a diamond-studded truncheon. As a token of May Day, his daughter sent the Queen a daisy of gold set with rubies.

In a similar manner, the denouement of Peele's *Arraignment of Paris* is centered upon courtly compliment and the presentation of a gift to Elizabeth. Here the same gods and goddesses who figured in the actual ceremonies of presentation assemble at the end of Peele's play and offer the golden apple to the regal spectator, Elizabeth herself, the paragon of all virtues.

In the mummeries and entertainments described above, usually a group of persons sent or brought gifts to the sovereign. In the related form of the lottery, also a pastime with which nobles entertained the visiting Queen, there were many recipients and one bestower of gifts. At a celebration presented in honor of the Queen by Sir Thomas Egerton at York House in 1601, a Mariner entered with a box of "trifles," and asked the ladies of the court to try their fortunes. Twenty-nine gifts were thus distributed, including a fan, bracelet, bodkin, and chain necklace. Each gift was accompanied by an appropriate fortune-telling verse, like the following "posy" attached to a prayer book:

> Your Fortune may prove good another day
> Till Fortune come, take you a booke to pray.

Five of the ladies received "blanks," i.e., verses without gifts.[35]

The denouement in *An Humorous Day's Mirth* is provided by this custom of giving gifts and applying them to the fortunes of the recipients. The lottery procession enters: " ... two with torches, the one of them Moren, then my Host and his Son, then his Maid drest like Queen Fortune with two pots in her hands." Amid the jesting interruptions common among courtiers enjoying an inept amateur show, the boy solemnly announces the advent of Fortune, "Dealing the lots/ Out of our pots." In Lemot's verses which accompany the gifts, the characters of the play find advice and moral instruction to cure their humors. Florilla's suspicious husband is told:

> Of all Fortune's friends, that hath joy in this life
> He is most happy that puts a sure trust in his wife.[36]

In these plays, both Peele and Chapman base their denouements upon devices drawn from the entertainments. As will be seen, Ben Jonson does likewise in *Every Man Out of His Humor* and justifies his ending by pointing out the precedent of the city pageants.

*   *   *

Literal-minded Elizabethans who witnessed royal entries upon the stage expected to see the accompanying ceremonies of welcome. Audience-minded playwrights met the problem by condensing the static oration or by turning it to dramatic effect. Subtly enriching the scenes or descriptions of royal receptions upon the Elizabethan stage was the image of loyal hearts reflected by true tongues. The humorous incongruity in amateur attempts at the classical oration was not overlooked by the playwrights, nor was the pretentious character who was invariably found participating in the welcome. Established forms for the eulogy of a prince, as taught in the schools and set forth in the handbooks, were followed in real life and upon the stage. At the estates visited by the Queen on progress, welcoming ceremonies and presentation of the gift were incorporated into playlets whose devices suggested a feature of the pastoral play and the denouements in *The Arraignment of Paris* and *An Humorous Day's Mirth*.

CHAPTER THREE

Pageants, Progresses, and Plays

PAGEANTS

CIT. Let Rafe come out on May day in the morning, and speak
upon a Conduit with all his Scarfs about him, and his
Feathers, and his Rings, and his Knacks.

BOY. Why sir, you do not think of our plot, what will become
of that then?

CIT. Why sir, I care not what become on't, I'll have him come
out, or I'll fetch him out my self, I'll have something done
in honor of the City:

.   .   .   .

Enter Rafe

RAFE. London, to thee I do present the merry Month of May,
Let each true Subject be content to hear me what I say:
From the top of Conduit head, as plainly may appear,
I will both tell my name to you, and wherefore I came here.[1]

Having commanded performances of his other stage favorites, the Citizen in *The Knight of the Burning Pestle* now
watches with delight as Rafe reenacts a city pageant. The
Citizen's enthusiasm suggests that the pageant was as much
in demand upon the stage as were romance and civic adven-
ture. If time or facilities were lacking—Beaumont's play dem-

onstrates that proper occasion was of little concern—audiences were served individual features of the pageants, or satisfied by descriptions and allusions. An accompanying feature of the royal entry, the Lord Mayor's Day, and other civic celebrations, the pageants were always mentioned when such occasions were staged. "Shows, Pageants, and sights of honour" celebrate Anne's coronation in *Henry VIII*,[2] while Gower in *Pericles* asks his hearers to imagine

> What pageantry, what feats, what shows,
> What minstrelsy and pretty din
> V, ii, 6f.

greeted the King on his entry into Mytilin.

In general, the term "pageant" is here used according to its definition in the Oxford English Dictionary as "A tableau, representation, allegorical device . . . erected on a fixed stage or carried in a moving car, as a public show . . . device, or temporary structure, exhibited as a feature of a public triumph or celebration." Our present-day equivalents are "floats," such as those displayed in inaugural and Mardi Gras parades. The usage of the term "pageant" as a staged representation celebrating a royal entry is exemplified by the contemporary description of the reception of Henry VII at York in 1486: "At the further Ende of Conyeux Strete was ordeyned another Stage with a Pageant, wherin King Davide stode armede and crownede . . . "[3]

It is also important to remember that other connotations of the word among sixteenth century Englishmen frequently colored the conception of the street pageant as presented or described. In the Middle Ages, "pageant" sometimes referred only to the wagon on which a show was presented. However, it became more generally applied to the entire exhibition—show and structure. By association, the term which identified a public tableau was useful as well to designate a similarly formal, tableau-like representation of a stage of life. This application of the word is found especially in the visual arts. For example, the medieval "Pageants of Richard Beauchamp" are sketches, perhaps designs for a set of panel paintings or tapestries, which illustrate such episodes in the life of the Earl of Warwick as his birth, baptism, knighthood and death. In arrangement and design, some of the illustrations bear a close resemblance to the pageants. Pageant IV, in its tableau-like depiction of the coronation of Jane as the Queen of Henry IV, represents a favorite setting of the street shows, the throne scene. Similarly, it is recorded in the 1557 edition of his works that Sir Thomas More in his youth devised for his father's house in London "a goodly hanging of fyne paynted clothe with nyne pageants and verses over every of those pageants." The first "pageant" depicted a child playing with a ball, and the following ones showed a young man riding over the child, then Venus and Cupid standing on the young man, next Age with Venus and Cupid under his feet, and the successive victories of Death over the old man, Fame over Death, Time over Fame, and finally "Lady Eternitee sitting in a chayre under a sumptious cloth of estate, crowned with an imperial crown and under her fete lay the picture of Time."[4]

It is this connotation of the word "pageant" as a vivid scene representative of a stage of life which prompts Jaques' catalog of the seven ages of man, in reply to Duke Senior's observation that

> This wide and universal theatre
> Presents more woful pageants than the scene
> Wherein we play in.
>
> II, vii, 137 ff.

In these lines, the Duke pictures simultaneous presentations on scattered stages, which method of presentation was characteristic of the city pageants. Also contained in this passage is the Elizabethan connotation of "pageant" as synonymous with "play," designating the imitation of life upon a stage. However, with its associations of tableau and symbolism, "pageant" is richer in implication for Jaques' reply. Like remembered events which present themselves to the mind in photographic "still" fashion, so "pageant" here strikingly suggests the suspension of movement in a swift revelation of the representative stopped scene before life resumes its course.

In its most literal sense, "pageant" to the Elizabethans meant a particular feature of the public celebration—the decorative, symbolic devices incorporating actors, properties and setting, and mounted upon city gates, landmarks, or temporary structures. Thus, the basic aim and ingredients for drama and pageant are the same—presentation of a theme by means of live actors, with appropriate properties and setting. The differences are attributable mainly to the factor of time. The two hours' traffic on the playhouse stage was often limited to ten minutes on the pageant arch. The necessarily visual and immediate appeal of the brief pageant accounted for its accent upon decoration and total design; when such effects were desired upon the stage, there existed a ready medium from which they could be borrowed.

Without the use of live actors in their display, the pageants probably would have had a negligible influence upon the drama. The employment of actors in the pageants may have evolved from the early custom of placing singing children in the towers of the city gates at a royal entry. This practice may in turn have had its origin in the tenth century Palm Sunday celebrations, wherein a procession, representing the entry into Jerusalem, would set forth from a hill outside the town, and as it entered the city gates, the choir boys stationed thereon would sing antiphonally, "gloria laus et honor . . . "[5] At later public celebrations of civic and royal occasions, when singing children were similarly placed, perhaps the physical height of their station suggested that they be costumed like angels. This practice persisted, for singing and music frequently accompanied the pageants. In 1487, Elizabeth, the wife of the first Tudor King, rode in coronation procession through London where, it was reported, "In dyvers Parts of the Citie were ordeynede wele singing Childerne. Some arrayde like Angells . . . "[6] In early civic festivities, other costumed actors participated, representing figures related to the occasion. Later, groups of such characters, historical, religious, allegorical, and mythological, were organized into *tableaux vivants*, and mounted upon the gates and landmarks.[7]

Thus, the pageant, with its striking visual effect produced by living actors in a decorative mounting, became a standard feature of all important civic or royal celebrations. More than mere showpieces, each pageant had a theme or message to carry to the sovereign and spectators. Because of the time limit, these themes were made explicit either by the comments of a narrator, or by rudimentary dialogue or dumb show on the part of the actors. Like illustrations for a courtesy book, the pageants displayed patterns of behavior for monarch and magistrate, for country and community.

Unlike the private masques, the pageants were completely public. In addition to their outdoor presentation, they were sponsored, and often planned and acted, by the people. As the form grew more elaborate, professional actors such as Edward Alleyn, and professional writers, like Peele, Munday and Jonson, were employed for the more lavish London displays. Yet the common denominator of all the entertainments —offerings of the towns visited on progress, the shows presented by the country people and the pageants displayed in London—was the earnest desire of the people themselves to demonstrate their good will toward the honored sovereign. Everyone shared in the preparations: the buildings were painted, and streets were cleaned and newly-gravelled. From the windows of their houses the townspeople hung decorations and painted cloths. So Fame describes to Elizabeth the joyful preparations of the citizens for welcoming her to Bristol in 1574:

> Then collors cast they o'er the walls,
> and deckt old housis gaye.[8]

New clothing was in order for all who could provide it, and the town officials were a show in themselves, in the full dress robes of their offices. In its decoration of the royal route and in the outfits of the citizens, the whole town of Sandwich in 1573 turned out in black and white, the official colors of the Queen's liveries.

The London citizens most frequently responsible for the presentation of the pageants were the guildsmen, who generally planned the shows and hired the writers to develop them and the actors to present them. In addition to their interest in civic welfare, the gentlemen of the guilds naturally responded to the advertising opportunities provided by the pageants. Notable examples of such promotion are provided by the Lord Mayors' Shows, whose decorations served to laud the organization, its products, and its members, who were accordingly assessed for this privilege. Such a subscription drive in action seems to be indicated in *The Three Lords and Three Ladies of London,* when Simplicity comes to collect from Diligence "Fourty pence and furniture by my Lord pompes pointment, against the wedding day: to bee one of the show-makers, I doe not say shoe-makers, and yet they be honest men."[9]

But while many a townsman had an active interest in the exhibits by reason of personal contribution, the show was the thing which appealed to the throng. Beaumont was not alone in observing that those who shoved and thrust for a better view of the street shows enjoyed seeing these devices repeated on the stage. Alert to the tastes of the paying audience, playwrights would generally thrust their critical barbs not at the pageant, but at the pageant-maker (whose fee was far in excess of the dramatist's). Anthony Munday, for instance, is satirized in *The Case is Altered* as Balladino, "Pageant Poet to the City. . . . when a worse cannot be had,"[10] and in *Histrimastix* as Posthaste, a "peaking Pagenter."[11]

Like the drama, the street shows developed greatly in the sixteenth century. This period saw a crystallization of the form and themes of the pageant, while increasing elaboration of the spectacular effects was evident. The choice of stations on which shows were displayed remained standard, as did the route which the sovereign took in passing through the city. The first pageant, or in cases of small towns the only one, was generally placed on a special stage or upon the entrance gate itself. Such a temporary stand was actually erected on the stage in *2 Promos and Cassandra,* with Phallax overseeing the construction:

> . . . up with the frame quickly,
> So space your roomes, as the nyne worthyes may,
> Be so instauld, as best may please the eye.
> I, iv

In London, the landmarks decorated included St. Paul's, the gates of Ludgate and Temple Bar, the Conduits in Cornhill and Fleet Street, the Great and Little Conduits, and the Standard and the Cross in Cheapside. The gates were particularly well adapted to the mounting of pageants as were the "conduits," or public reservoirs and fountains. These conduits were generally low, castellated buildings enclosing a cistern from which water issued. Stow records of the Conduit in Fleet Street, built in 1478, "this cesterne at the Standard they builded, and on the same a fayre tower of stone, garnished with images of S. Christopher on the top, and Angels round

about lower down . . . "[12] Such stone figures, which also embel
lished other landmarks and the city gates, blended with the
living allegorical figures of the pageants. And when the gates
were remodeled, the pageants undoubtedly contributed sug-
gestions for the new decorations. Aldgate, for instance, rebuilt
in 1609, displayed in a large square on the second level of
the east façade a figure of James I with a lion and unicorn
at his feet. On the highest level of the west façade was represented Fortune standing on a globe, and beneath, statues of
Charity and Peace.[13]

A show mounted upon an arch or city gate generally utilized three levels, with the main tableau mounted on the space
above the archways, further decorations at the very top,
and below the main show, a stand for the speaker, placed low
enough so that he could be heard. The top-most level, which
might contain carved, mechanical or living figures, or scenic
representations, was also the ideal location for the depiction
of heaven, with God's throne and angel-choristers. The main
show on the second level might take the form of a flat painting (such as that of Henry VII and James in 1603-4) explained
by living actors standing at the sides or below. As was more
often the case, the main show might display a tableau of
actors, grouped with properties against scenery.

The effect of a pageant mounted upon a conduit is presented by the opening scenes of Peele's *David and Bethsabe*.
Here a device resembling a conduit may have been employed
to represent Bethsabe's bath and David's tower in scene one
and the actual conduit and tower referred to in scene two.
At the beginning of the play, Prologue "drawes a curtaine
and discouers Bethsabe with her maid bathing ouer a spring
. . . Dauid sits aboue vewing her" from "his Princely tower."
The grouping, with a tableau on the lower level and the
throned figure above, suggests the familiar façade of the pageant mounted on the conduit, with its fountain beneath and

battlements above. In the second scene, Urias and his train come on with drum and ensign ready to siege Rabbath. Since the building background again represents the tower and fountain, it is to be inferred that the continued association of the two is required by stationary scenery or desired by a playwright who wishes to repeat a striking effect. The leader calls on his men:

> First . . . Let us assault and scale this kingly Tower,
> Where all their conduits and their fountaines are . . .
> ii, 187 ff.

The conduit-tower is not found in the Biblical source, *Samuel,* where it is recorded simply that "David sent Joab and they besieged Rabbath."

In his study of the influence of the pageant on the physical stage, George Kernodle has considered the debt to show-architecture of the three-level façade of the English stage, with its inner and upper stages for tableau effects and settings similar to those of the pageant. He concludes that "the pattern of the Elizabethan stage was established in the *tableaux vivants.*"[14]

Combining carved figures, flat paintings, and living actors with physical properties, the street shows presented their themes by dumb show, dialogue, or narration. With the display frequently arranged on two or three levels, the topmost space would be reserved for merely decorative figures, panto-mimic action might take place on the middle level, and dialogue usually was confined to the street or a lower stage, where additional actors might be exhibited in tableau. Frequently a special stand, in the lower position, was erected for the expositor. The structures were further ornamented by forms or pictures placed in niches or arcades on the façade, while any remaining blank spaces were covered with living, carved, or painted figures, with scrolls bearing mottoes, with properties, and with verses. The insides of the archways were likewise decorated. Sometimes the pageant, draped with silken curtains, was not to be seen until the king arrived with his procession. At that moment, the curtains dropped and revealed the splendid show. Pageants were exhibited not only on gates, conduits and landmarks, but also on specially-built stages, and on permanent architectural structures which had been altered for the occasion. To exhibit simpler shows, one-level stands were constructed, resembling the pageant wagon of the morality and mystery plays. Sometimes platform and façade were combined.

Upon gates, arches and stages, then, the people saw as a main attraction a group of actors dressed and propertied appropiately as historical, Biblical, allegorical, legendary or mythological characters, arranged formally within a setting. When the ruler's procession arrived at the pageant, the characters might recite verses explaining the show and applying it to current conditions. Sometimes the actors would remain mute, while an expositor related the significance of the tableau. By 1604, this exposition of the pageant had in some instances become so extensive that Ben Jonson, in his account of James' entry in that year, felt it necessary to take the showmakers to task for their vigor in explaining the pageant so often and in such detail. Not only did the narrator and the properties identify the figures; in addition, the characters in the pageants, like those in tapestries, frequently bore their names on scrolls below their feet or above their heads, or on tablets worn about their necks. For example, a pageant at Elizabeth's coronation explicitly identified Truth and her properties, and pointed out her relationship to the other characters in the show:

. . . directly over her head was set her name and tytle, in Latin and Englyshe, 'Temporis filia,' 'The Daughter of

Plate III. The Garden of Plenty Pageant presented at the royal entry of James I to London, 1604.

Plate IV. The war-peace theme of the pageants as used by Rubens' Temple of Janus at the entry of Prince Ferdinand to Antwerp, 1642.

Tyme'. . . . And on her brest was written her proper name, whiche was 'Veritas,' 'Trueth,' who helde a booke in her hande, upon the which was written 'Verbum Veritatis,' 'The Woorde of Trueth.'[15]

Through the decorated city streets, from one pageant to another, wound the colorful royal procession. On occasion, one of the characters might come down from the show into the street, like Sylvanus at James' entry, to lead the ruler and spectators to the next exhibit. This procedure is reminiscent of that in such medieval guild plays as the Digby *Conversion of St. Paul,* where Saul, going on progress to Damascus "rydyth forth with hys seruantes a-bowt the place," and a character serving as Poeta asks the audience to "follow . . . this generall processyon," to the next stage, which represents Damascus.[16]

James' royal entry and coronation celebration, long postponed because of the plague, represent the most elaborate development of many of the themes expressed by similar shows throughout the sixteenth century. Following the usual pattern of the welcomes, the first device, which was unperformed, was to have presented the Genius of the City, St. George of England and St. Andrew of Scotland applauding their "league of unitie," and greeting James:

Dread King, our hearts make good, what words do want,
To bid thee boldly enter Troynovant.

The King and the attendant throng could not have failed to be impressed by the first "arch of triumph," designed by Ben Jonson and erected at Fenchurch. Upon the appearance of the "sun," James, a silk curtain which was painted to depict a heavy cloud dropped and revealed at the top of the arch a representation of the houses, towers and steeples of London. The main tableau presented a galaxy of civic ideals. Monarchia Britannica, with Divine Wisdom at her feet, sat enthroned above the Genius of the City, with Gladnesse, Veneration, Promptitude, Vigilance, Loving Affection, and Unanimity grouped on a spreading ascent. On a lower level lay the river god Thamesis, who was aroused by the Genius of the City to celebrate the King.

The Italians' pageant which followed was as decorative in appearance, but simpler in theme. By means of a large painting, which depicted Henry VII handing a scepter to King James, this arch demonstrated James' rightful succession to the throne. His own descendants were the subject of the decorations on the interior of the archway, painted on both sides with olive and palm trees, whose abundance was wished to James and his family.

Next his Majesty witnessed an arch erected by London residents from another foreign country. To these Dutchmen, pageantry offered an excellent opportunity for promoting trade. On one side of the arch, curtains parted to reveal seventeen young damsels bearing appropriate coats of arms and representing Belgia's seventeen provinces.[17] On the other side, were painted the Dutch people working at their chief industries—men, women and children beating and carding hemp, and spinning and weaving; burghers buying and selling, and mariners fishing and shipping.

For the following pageant, Thomas Dekker created a readily comprehensible allegory in pantomime. An actor portraying Arabia Britannica leaned sadly on a mound, while Detraction and Oblivion slept beside the trickling Fountain of Vertue. But as James appeared, Fame sounded her trumpet, and Detraction and Oblivion, in "the glorious presence of the King ... were suddenly thereby daunted, and sunke downe." The fountain sprang up vigorously with "milke, wine, and balme." Circumspection, who had foreseen this "blessed tyme," acted as narrator and interpreted the "dumbe mysterie."

Again James observed his beneficial effect upon the Kingdom in the next device, the Garden of Plenty, where a flour-ishing commonwealth was represented by a bower garnished with apples, pears, roses, lilies, and other fruits and flowers "most artificially molded to the life." (See Plate III) . Here sat actors representing Peace and Plenty, attended by Gold, Sil-ver, Pomona, Ceres and the nine muses and the seven liberal arts, all of whom throve, invigorated by the reign of another "sun"

> Whose new beames make our Spring,
> Men glad, and birdes to sing . . .

Probably feeling by that time far from paragon-like, James arrived at Fleet Street to behold a tableau exhibiting his ideal attributes. Highest sat his chief virtue, Justice, represented by Astraea. Then Vertue was enthroned above Fortune, be-neath whose feet revolved the world, to imply that "His Majestie's fortune was above the world, but his vertues above his fortune." The globe beneath Fortune's feet displayed the estates placed in order, to represent the Golden World. To one side, stood the villain of the show, Envy, feeding on ad-ders' heads and eyeing James' four cardinal virtues and his four kingdoms. An actor representing Zeal, the restorer of order among the estates, explained the pageant.

According to the pageants, James was not only the bringer of peace and plenty and the model of virtue, but he equalled Vergil's ideal monarch—Augustus. Ben Jonson's show in the Strand, in a setting of a rainbow, the moon, sun and the Pleiades, depicted Electra "hanging in the ayre, in figure of a Comet." The goddess related how she fled at the fall of Troy, to return now to usher in James' golden reign, and compared herself to the comet

> . . . that did auspicate
> So lasting glory to Avgvstvs' state.

The last arch, also by Jonson, celebrated the new Augustus by presenting the Temple of Janus, to which Vergil alludes in praising the Roman Emperor and the age of peace. In this pageant, the figures of Peace, Liberty, Safety and Felicity each trod upon a vanquished foe—Mars, Servitude, Danger, and Unhappiness, respectively. Meanwhile, at the altar of the temple, the Genius of London sacrificed the heart of the city to James, after which the gates of the temple closed, to signify a reign of peace.[18] (Cf. Plate IV).

A dual purpose is revealed in each of these exhibits at James' entry: to please the King and spectators by a splendid show and to instruct them by a moral embodied within that show. From the earliest days, the city pageants combined visual appeal and symbolical significance to express themes as traditional as that of loyalty in the welcoming oration. Participated in, sponsored and viewed by the citizens themselves, the shows were an index of public opinion concerning the nation and its ruler.

Then, as now, the citizens' ideal commonwealth was one of peace and plenty. Thus, at James' entry, the Garden of Plenty show depicted such a country, in which industry, agriculture and arts flourished, while the Temple of Janus pageant compared James and the peace-loving Augustus. The same ideal was presented in Marston's *Histriomastix,* which also employed the pageants' device of presenting an enthroned personified abstraction *en tableau* with companion virtues or vices. In this manner, *Histriomastix* depicted the commonwealth under the reign of Peace and Plenty, and then under the successive rules of Pride and Envy, resulting in the sway of War and Poverty. The dreaded villains were always War and Dissension. The entertainment presented before the Queen at Bristol in 1574 was not only an exciting water show, but it also demonstrated the vulnerability of the Fort of Feeble Pollicie, which was attacked by War at the instigation of wily Dissension. These personifications of Peace, Plenty, War and Dissension represented vivid symbols with which to express the hardships of the past, and the hopes for the future. So Richmond, who is about to be crowned Henry VII at the end of *Richard III,* employs the personified abstractions and the symbolic red and white roses of the pageants to voice his wish for union, peace, and prosperity:

> We will unite the White Rose and the Red.
> .   .   .   .
> And let their heirs (God, if thy will be so)
> Enrich the time to come with smooth-fac'd peace,
> With smiling plenty, and fair prosperous days!
>   V, v, 19 ff.

Richmond's personification of "smiling plenty" was only one way to represent this ideal state of the nation. Sometimes, more immediate than a personified abstraction or a symbolic garden, the demonstration took the form of a display of prospering trades, like one phase of modern advertising. For example, in 1578, when the Queen went to Norwich, she witnessed a pageant in which child actors presented the various aspects of the wool trade, such as spinning, knitting and weaving. Painted panels illustrated and identified the several types of looms. At James' entry, a similar commercial exhibit was incorporated in the Dutchmen's pageant which depicted the trades and occupations of the provinces of Belgia.

Shows advertising a flourishing trade might also take the opportunity to remind the ruler of the country's obligation to protect this commerce. Thus the exciting and popular water siege was frequently concerned with a pirate attack upon a merchant vessel which required the aid of a Government ship. On progress in 1573, Elizabeth witnessed such a mock sea battle at Orpington, and at Sandwich she watched a water assault on a fort where the fight featured a duel between two actors on separate ships. At Bristol in the following year, the allegorical water show of Dissension, Feeble Policy and Peace took place. Many of the devices of these shows were employed in the elaborate water fete at Elvetham to present a national theme, celebrating the victory over the Armada.

Sea-pageantry was to be found too on the Thames, which was decorated by the barges of the prosperous guilds as a customary feature of the annual Lord Mayor's festivities.[19] In the colorful water procession to Westminster for the sovereign's confirmation of the new official's appointment, the resplendent barge of the Mayor was accompanied by others trimmed with colorful scarfs and displaying allegorical characters. Perhaps Shakespeare had in mind such splendor upon the Thames when he referred in *The Merchant of Venice* to "pageants of the sea,"[20] and in *Othello* to the fleet as "a pageant to keep us in false gaze."[21]

That water pageantry was popular in London on occasions other than Lord Mayors' Shows is evidenced by the celebration of Anne Boleyn's coronation, when merchants fitted out company barges which were almost as splendid as Cleopatra's. Upon the occasion of the visit of King Christian of Denmark, James gave the visiting sovereign a barge of his own, "fashioned like a tower or little castle ... all close with glasse windowes, and casements faire carued guilt ... the roofe ... made with battlements, pynacles, and pyramides." In reciprocation, the Danish ruler honored his host by presenting on the Thames a firework-pageant of the burning of the Deadly Sins. One interesting feature of the show is that it represents solely the negative side of a subject which is conventional in pageants —the virtues of the ideal sovereign. Instead of what Spenser termed "polliticke vertues," this show depicted the vices of

a public official—Extravagance, Deceit and Injustice, along
with five of the conventional Seven Deadly Sins. Presented on
the Thames, "not withstanding the brightness of the sonne,"
as reported by Stow,

The Deuice of wild fire was in pageant wise, betweene
foure round pillers, vppon a lighter framed, where the seuen
deadly sinnes in their liuely colours, shape: and Caracters,
sate chained fast, and for their wickednesse bound to endure
eternall punishment, and ouer their heads in the midest of
them, vppon the top of a pinacle was a firece Lion cowchaunt,
signifying sudden vengeance . . . and from the Lyons mouth
the fire first did issue forth, and . . . descended into all parts
. . . with loftie Rocketts, and fire flakes mounting in the ayre
. . . and for the space of more then a quarter of an hower, the
foresaid Images sate burning in Etnaes flame . . .

Appropriate words were painted above each of the figures,
in the fashion of the tapestries and pageants. Injustitia's lines
were:

> Quid leges, Quid jura vetent, nil curo, nec aequum
> Quid fiet; arbitrii lex mihi sola placet.[22]

The display of monarchial vices was, of course, neither a
favorite nor a safe theme. More often, the ruler was con-
fronted with shows in which the citizens hopefully displayed
the ideal attributes for a monarch. For example, when the
boy king Henry VI returned to London from his coronation
in Paris in 1432, he was welcomed by a display presenting a
child ruler surrounded by the virtues of Mercy, Truth and
Clemency. This form of allegorical advice-giving, or at least
of wishful thinking, became an established practice. At Elizabeth's entry, a child representing the Queen sat on the throne
of Worthy Governance which was supported by Pure Religion,
Love of Subjects, Wisdom and Justice, while a pageant celebrating James' coronation likewise extolled his Justice.

Related to such royal entry displays are the Lord Mayors' Shows which exhibited the virtues expected of a magistrate. Sometimes this theme was treated in a pageant containing figures of outstanding Lord Mayors of the past, and recalling their special services to the city and to the sovereign. In 1590, the Fishmonger's show presented a notable collection, including not only such personifications as The Peace of England, Wisdom, Pollicie, God's Truth, Plentie, Loialtie, Concord, Commonwealth, Science and Labor, but also the characters of Richard II and Jack Straw. The basic elements of a plot are necessarily presented in this show by exposition rather than action. Richard asks the help of Lord Mayor William Walworth, represented by Commonwealth, to "daunt the rebel's pride." Jack Straw reports that he was "tamd" by Walworth, who then announces:

> I slewe Jacke Straw, who sought my Kings disgrace
>
> . . . .
>
> Thus did the King with honors me adore
> And Fame herself still laudeth me therefore.[23]

Undoubtedly such Lord Mayors' Pageants were instrumental in promoting the guildsman as hero in novels and dramas. About 1592 the play of *Jack Straw* with Walworth as its leading character was produced, to be followed by Deloney's novels, and plays like Dekker's *The Shoemaker's Holiday*.

Thus in the Lord Mayors' Shows, the international Nine Worthies of history are replaced by the local Worthies of the guilds. Around the time London burghers were applauding *Jack Straw* on the stage, Richard Johnson brought out a book "pleasant for Gentlemen, not unseemely for Magistrates and most profitable for Prentises." Reminiscent of the street shows, his *Nine Worthies of London* which went through two editions in the year of its issue, depicted the allegorical figures of Fame and Clio calling upon the deceased ancient worthies of the city to rise from an Elysian bank, where they rested arm-in-arm, to stand forth, identify themselves, and deliver their stories in verse. Johnson included Walworth as a representative of the Fishmongers' guild, while other worthies represented the Grocers, Vintners, Merchant Taylors, Mercers and Silk Weavers.[24] Perhaps the best known of the guildsmen-heroes, Simon Eyre in *The Shoemaker's Holiday*, colorfully displays his disdain for some of the Worthies of history as compared with his journeyman, Ralph:

Hector of Troy was an hackney to him, Hercules and Termagant scoundrelles, Prince Arthurs Round Table, by the Lord of Ludgate, nere fed such a tall, such a dapper swordman.[25]

In 2 *If You Know Not Me,* Heywood takes a hint from the pageants which exhibited outstanding former mayors as examples to civic leaders. Here, Dr. Nowell leads his guests—Gresham, Ramsey, Lady Ramsey and Hobson—on an after-dinner tour of the gallery, where he keeps pictures of "charitable Citizens,"

That hauing fully fatisfied [sic] your bodyes,
You may by them learne to refresh your soules.
vi, 759 ff.

In the tradition of the pageant, Nowell displays pictures of such past mayors as Sir John Filpot and Richard Whittington, and tells of their good deeds. So affected is Gresham that, with tears in his eyes, he resolves to do good for the city and its inhabitants, the resolution materializing in his construction of the Royal Exchange.

This practice of displaying painted pictures seems to have been carried over from the pageant to the playhouse. An important medium for decorating the street shows, paintings sometimes supplanted the *tableaux vivants,* as they did in certain shows at the coronation celebrations of King Philip of Spain and James I. Like *If You Know Not Me,* the play *Dido,* by Marlowe and Nashe, employs the display of heroes' pictures,[26] and in the Dekker-Marston *Satiromastix,* two portraits are presented for a comparison between the real Horace and his impersonator.[27] The representation of the pictures of Hamlet's father and uncle in Act III, scene iv, may have accorded with this convention of exhibiting paintings of former and present worthies. Thus original stage tradition may very likely be reflected in the often-censured illustration in Rowe's edition[28] which depicts upon the wall in Gertrude's room portraits of both the past and present kings, to which Hamlet refers:

> Look here upon this picture, and on this,
> The counterfeit presentment of two brothers.
> > III, iv, 53 f.

Modern productions have favored the use of two miniatures, the former king's worn by Hamlet and Claudius' by Gertrude.

In the pageants, living likeness of the worthies—whether civic, national, or international—undoubtedly had more appeal than painted representations. As models of conduct to be adopted or avoided by monarch or magistrate, these characters were drawn from history and the Bible, as well as from allegory and civic life. At Queen Elizabeth's coronation, Deborah was exhibited as a precedent for the Queen. The judge and restorer of the house of Israel was depicted consulting with two members each of the nobility, the clergy and the commonwealth. As the example to be shunned, the tyrant Nero overthrown by Justice was displayed in a pageant at Edinburgh in 1503 honoring Margaret Tudor and James IV. Sometimes it was felt that a mere exhibition of an historical or legendary figure was not forceful enough, and the characters themselves addressed advice to the ruler. At Norwich in 1578, Esther warned Elizabeth of the dangers of fraud as well as of force, and cautioned her to beware of the smiling looks of enemies. As did the dramas on civic themes, the chronicle plays surely received impetus from the pageants, which had earlier staged portrayals of historical characters by live actors.[29]

The advice which the street shows offered frequently concerned the general behavior of an ideal prince; sometimes it dealt with problems more specific and personal. As did *Gorboduc,* a pageant might remind the ruler of the necessity of establishing a clear succession to the crown. At her coronation festivities, Anne Boleyn was greeted by a pageant which celebrated a future heir to the throne by displaying St. Ann with her issue and Mary Cleophas, with her four children. The show of Zabeta, prepared for presentation at Kenilworth but for obvious reasons not exhibited, carries a very outspoken message to Queen Elizabeth from her host, Leicester. As the messenger of Juno, goddess of wedlock, Iris was to stress upon the nymph Zabeta the importance of marriage, and to implore her to foresake allegiance to the chaste Diana:

> How necesserie were for worthy Queenes to wed
> That know you wel, whose life alwaies in learning
>   hath beene led.[30]

Even more concerned with the present succession than with future ones, the street shows provided a graphic and effective means of assuring the public of the new sovereign's rightful title to the throne. Such demonstrations displayed famous ancestors, amid an assortment of the standard symbols of genealogy—trees, vines, plants, and heraldic animals. At Elizabeth's coronation, her legitimate claim to the throne was depicted in a show utilizing the roses of Lancaster and York, a favorite pageant device for symbolizing a united country. A red rose enclosing a figure of Henry VII and a white rose with

his wife Elizabeth branched into one flower which displayed
Henry VIII and Anne Boleyn. From there, a single branch
led to the top of the plant, where Queen Elizabeth was represented. Claimant to the crowns of both England and France,
Henry VI was honored in 1432 by a pageant exhibiting a
tower which was decorated with the arms of the respective
countries and was flanked by two green trees with the representations of the pedigrees of St. Edward and St. Louis. By
1486, Henry himself was being represented as a historical
worthy in a pageant at Worcester, where he hailed his nephew
and cousin Henry VII as his successor. In turn, Henry VII's
grandson, Edward VI, witnessed in 1547 a street show in
which his rightful succession was elaborately represented by
the heraldic phoenix and lion, as well as by red and white
roses. As a literal accompaniment to the symbolism of these
pageants of genealogy, the lineage of the new ruler was recited by presenters and recorded on decorative scrolls on the
façade.

In the history plays are to be found similarly undramatic
passages which set forth a claimant's genealogical right to
the throne. In *Sir John Oldcastle,* Scroop asks,

> Once more my Lord of Cambridge make rehersal
> How you do stand intiteled to the Crowne.

In reply, Cambridge, with the help of Scroop, details for
thirty-eight lines his own family tree and that of his wife.[31]
While the drama's incorporation of these passages, whose
source was the chronicle, may seem artificial and static to us,
the Elizabethan audience was conditioned by the pageants
of genealogy, and was accustomed to such demonstrations.
Perhaps the cataloging of ancestors was carried over, along
with the historical figures, from the street shows. Frequently,
such speeches were enlivened in the plays by decorative imagery drawn from genealogical symbolism made popular by

the pageants. In the Temple Garden Scene in 1 *Henry VI,*
Warwick proclaims York's title to the throne as follows:

> His grandfather was Lionel Duke of Clarence,
> Third son to the third Edward, King of England.
> Spring crestless yeomen from so deep a root?
>   II, iv, 83 ff.

The most colorful ancestor claimed by Henry VII and his
descendants was the historic-legendary King Arthur, whose
prophecy that he would return helped to enforce a somewhat
questionable claim to the crown.[32] Thus, the exhibition of
King Arthur became a requisite at celebrations honoring the
Tudor sovereigns. For example, the Janitor in a pageant at
Worcester was to have welcomed Henry VII as Arthur, the
true King of Britain and defense of England, and the entertainments at Kenilworth were based upon the Arthurian
legends. Both as English worthy and ancestor, King Arthur
was displayed in a show celebrating the visit of Emperor
Charles V to Henry VIII, and the chivalric king continued
to be exhibited throughout the sixteenth century as one of
the Nine Worthies. With the accession of the Stuarts, it was
opportunely discovered that King Arthur was also an ancestor of James I.

An effective medium for civic and political propaganda,
the pageant likewise served the Reformation in England.
Throughout the sixteenth century, Catholic countries like
Spain and Italy continued to present pageants concerning
the Virgin and the Trinity, while in England the public
shows reflected the religious policies of the ruler. After his
break with the Church, Henry VIII was entertained by a
water show in which his own forces defeated those of the
Pope. According to Foxe, Mary had ordered the words "Verbum Dei" obliterated from the Bible carried by Henry VIII
in a painting of the Nine Worthies which was to be displayed

at the entry of Philip of Spain. The Bible also figured in a pageant celebrating Elizabeth's coronation. Here, Truth or true religion, who had been in hiding during Mary's reign, came forth with her father, Time, to present the English Bible to the Queen.

During the period of the Armada, as foreign war threatened and nationalism grew, a new theme became prevalent in the street shows and plays—the celebration of the isle of England as an impregnable fortress. In true Renaissance fashion, pride was asserted in England not only as a power in the sixteenth-century world, but as a country of honorable antiquity. Pageants of the period reminded the Englishmen and their visitors from abroad of Britain's Trojan ancestor, Brutus, who founded the New Troy and fought the giants inhabiting the isle before the Romans came.

In the current of popular opinion as reflected in the pageants, the citizens' ideal was peace, plenty and true religion, under a just and rightful ruler, in a strong and prominent country. Since all of these ideas which are treated later in the drama were first expressed in a similar medium in the street shows, it is safe to assume that the drama looked to the pageant for figures, symbols and devices with which to state these common themes. At times, therefore, the dramatic presentation unmistakeably resembled that of the pageant. For instance, the Temple Garden Scene in 1 *Henry VI* must have reminded the audience of a pageant on the evils of civil dissension. Here in a garden setting of symbolic red and white roses, the dialogue is formal and the movement patterned as the two sides are formed: Richard, Warwick, Vernon and Lawyer, against Somerset and Suffolk. At the end of the scene, in the manner of the pageant presenter, Warwick makes a riming application:

> . . . this brawl to-day

Grown to this faction in the Temple Garden
Shall send, between the Red Rose and the White,
A thousand souls to death and deadly night.
II, iv, 124 ff.

Thus, when the drama utilized certain themes associated with
the street shows, it also borrowed from the pageant's method
of presentation, as evidenced not only by common properties
and symbols, but also by the dumb shows and tableau effects
on the Elizabethan stage.

THE INEXPLICABLE DUMB SHOW

IN *The Case is Altered,* when Balladino is bragging of his
accomplishments as "Pageant Poet to the city," he is reminded
that he has been cited "in print already for the best plotter."
Desirous of recognition as a pageanteer as well, he replies,
"I might as well ha bene put in for a dumb shew too."[33] The
terms "dumb show" and "pageant" were sometimes synonymous, then, to the Elizabethans, and a relationship between
the two forms has been suggested previously by scholars. Willard Farnham has pointed out that the dumb shows in *Gorboduc* are related to the city pageants,[34] while George Kernodle
has stated that the English dumb show is analogous to the
Italian *intermedio,* both forms having received impetus
from the pageants.[35] Certainly, the pageant and the dumb
show are similar in their employment of symbolism to state a
theme. More specifically, likenesses appear in properties,
characters, themes, and techniques. Playing time in the pageant was about equal to that in the dumb show.

As introduced into English drama by *Gorboduc,* the dumb
show served varying functions: sometimes it symbolized a
general moral to be drawn from the act it preceded, as in the

first dumb show in *Gorboduc,* where the weakness of a divided kingdom is indicated by a bundle of sticks which is unbreakable until the sticks are handed around separately and then easily broken. In the last dumb show in *Jocasta,* Fortune, her feet on a ball representing the globe of the world, changes the places of the two kings on her right hand with the two slaves on her left, thus pointing the moral of the final act and expressing the theme of the play—the unsteady fortunes of all men, be they sovereigns or slaves. Other dumb shows might foreshadow action to be unfolded in the following act, as does the funeral procession in the second dumb show in *Jocasta.* As exemplified in such later dramas as *The White Devil* and *Pericles* [36] a third use was to indicate important incidents omitted from the regular action. Finally, the dumb show merges with the drama, and develops into effective moments of pantomime within the play itself.[37]

The dumb shows on the Elizabethan stage bore the same resemblance to the Italian *intermedii* as the English pageants did to those of Italy. Pageants not only in England and Italy, but also in France, Spain and the Netherlands employed similar properties, symbols, and themes, which were used as well by the respective dumb shows and *intermedii.* Most of the difference between the pageants of the various countries can be attributed to the aim, the audience, or the degree of technical accomplishment in the presentation. Since close examination reveals that many of the differences between the two stage forms reflect similar differences in the pageants of England and Italy, it seems reasonable to assume a native influence from pageant to dumb show or *intermedio* in the two respective countries. The scenic splendor of the Italian pageants left its mark on the *intermedio* which, like the English masque, strove to produce an effect of beauty by mechanically ingenious scenery. The dumb show, like the English pageant and procession, sought a pleasing visual effect in the grouping or formal movement of costumed characters with symbolical properties, and expressed a moral or political thesis by means of this spectacle.

The form of entr'acte entertainment was conditioned by circumstances varying in England from those in Italy. Associated with comedy in Italy until 1566, the *intermedii* served to enliven the intermissions with spectacular dances of allegorical or legendary figures. Sometimes these shows had political import, as indicated by one which accompanied a comedy by Nicola Grassi in 1513 and represented a lamenting Italy despoiled by barbarians. A few days later, the same *intermedio* appeared in another comedy by another author, Guidobaldo Rugiero, depicting the maid Italy as rescued by the Duke of Urbino, who appeared with morris dancers to drive away the barbarians and replace the crown on her head.[38] In 1539, for the comedy *Il Commodo,* there were successive *intermedii* of shepherds, nymphs and tritons, Silenus and Amazons. In an *intermedio* in 1589 for *La Pellegrina,* a mountain was raised, representing Parnassus, with eighteen nymphs upon it; then the set divided, to reveal two dark caverns, whence musicians issued.[39] Usually, the connection with the play was nebulous. Even from these few examples, it can be seen that the Italian shows with their stress upon the dance and upon scenic effects, resemble more the private English masque than the public dumb show.

Like the pageants, the English dumb shows incorporated splendor with symbolism, visual with mental appeal. Perhaps taking a hint from the street shows, English playwrights discovered that the stage shows might present a moral or political theme which carried the universal application characteristic of the pageants, and also was relevant to the plot at hand. The first dumb show in *Gorboduc* expresses a recurrent pageant theme—the evils of a divided kingdom. As he frequently does in the pageants, the familiar figure of the wild man here represents the early, uncivilized inhabitants of England before the kingdom was established by Brute, who divided it among his sons. The second dumb show presented a good counselor offering the king a drink in a plain cup and an evil counselor offering him poison in a jeweled cup. With its balanced grouping, symbolism and political implications, this show is reminiscent of similar effects in pageants which gave advice to the sovereign. The evil and good counselors are, of course, characteristic of the plays of Seneca, and seem also to be related to the good and bad angels of the moralities. Yet it is the pageant, the forerunner not only of the dumb show with political significance, but also of such morality plays as *Magnificence* and *Respublica*, which first presents as hero not Everyman but the Commonwealth or the King.

In the Elizabethan drama of the 1580's and 90's, the dumb shows assimilated even more of the technique and subject matter of the pageant. A favorite pageant theme, the ideal of peace and plenty as opposed to war, became the subject of the second dumb show in *The Misfortunes of Arthur*. Here, Mordred is offered a cornucopia, a golden olive branch, and a sheaf of corn by three nymphs representing three offers from Arthur for peace and plenty. Mordred refuses them, and is chased by an Irishman representing Revenge and Fury of War.

Dumb shows concerned with religious issues employed standard characters and themes of the pageants. Besides its interesting relationship to Book I of *The Faerie Queene,* the Show of Truth at Elizabeth's coronation parade bears a resemblance to the opening dumb show of Dekker's *Whore of Babylon*.[40] In the pageant celebrating Elizabeth's entry, Truth, representing true religion, who had been hiding in a cave during Mary's reign, came forth with Father Time and delivered the Bible to Elizabeth. Dekker's dumb show employs the same characters and action, Truth and Time, and the presentation of the Bible, to express the same theme—the coming of

Elizabeth to the throne and the restoration of Protestantism. In a later dumb show in the same play, good triumphs over evil in the brief, graphic fashion of the pageant. Falsehood emerges from her cave, summons Campeius, a Friar, and three Gentlemen, but Time, Truth and Plain Dealing enter to thwart the evil plot to destroy true religion.

The coronation pageant exemplified, and perhaps prompted, the use of this particular symbol of Time and Truth to designate Elizabeth's restoration of Protestantism. In his *Choice of Emblems*, 1586, Geoffrey Whitney modified an emblem to accord with this sentiment. The source of his emblem was Junius' book of 1565, which had depicted "Truth the daughter of Time issuing forth from a cave, a three-fold plague appears to overwhelm: Strife, Envy and Slander." Junius' motto for this emblem had been "Truth by Time is revealed; by Discord is buried."[41] Whitney, however, changed the verses and the implication to represent not an attack upon, but a triumph of Truth with the assistance of Time. In Whitney's emblem, Envy, Strife, and Slander had enclosed Truth in a dungeon. from which Time had freed her. (See Plate V). The motto was changed to the following:

Thoughe strife make fier, thoughe Enuie eate her harte,
The innocent though Slaunder rente, and spoile:
Yet Time will comme, and take this ladies parte
And breake her bandes, and bring her foes to foile.[42]

The same pageant seems to have influenced the dumb show of Elizabeth's dream in Heywood's 1 *If You Know Not Me,* a play undoubtedly based upon chronicle accounts which contained these details of the royal entry. In the dream, Elizabeth's enemies, Winchester, Constable and Barwick, enter at one door, accompanied by Friars who attempt to kill her, but are thwarted by two angels who enter at another door to save her. As did Truth in the pageant, one of these angels

"opens the Bible and puts it in her hand as she sleepes."
Elizabeth awakens, discovers the book, and makes a comment
similar to the Queen's when she received the Bible at the
coronation. Here, the motto-like remark might serve as the
application of the dumb show:

> . . . heauen I trust
> With his eternall hand, will guide the iust.
>
> xiv, 1062 f.

Her royal entry at the end of the play follows the chronicle
accounts, for Elizabeth actually is presented with a Bible,
which she reverently kisses.

Strangely modern in this respect, the Elizabethan dramatists sought to represent dreams by symbolism and patterned
movements just as do our surrealistic motion pictures. Therefore, the dumb show with its pageant-like symbolism and
mannered action, as in *If You Know Not Me,* was especially
well-suited to the depiction of dreams and visions. In the
dumb show of Endymion's dream in Lyly's play, three ladies
enter, one of whom bears a knife and looking glass and attempts to stab the hero, but is restrained; then, as in the Tar-
quin legend, an old man offers a three-leaved book to Endymion who refuses it, while the man tears out the first two
sheets. Accepting the third sheet, Endymion sees the dangers
which beset the court, explained later as personifications of
Ingratitude, Treachery, and Envy—all characters long familiar to the pageant. "The strangest pageant, fashion'd like
a court," is reported to have been witnessed by Crites in his
dream in *Cynthia's Revels.* Unlike those in Endymion's dream,
the evils here concern affectations of courtiers rather than
dangers to the commonwealth, and are demonstrated by a
procession of court figures in dumb show fashion, which
Crites describes: "Here, stalkes me by a proud, and spangled
sir . . . "[43]

Just as the makers of the early motion pictures unconsciously and unnecessarily confined themselves to many of the limitations of the legitimate stage, so the Elizabethan playwrights, often involuntarily, carried over to the more flexible stage many of the conventions of the older pageant. One manifestation of this can be seen in the dumb shows, a form whose accepted non-realism provided a great latitude for imagination and fancy. Instead, the situations, characters, and properties almost invariably are limited to those employed earlier by the pageants. Thus, some of the properties characteristic of pageant and dumb show include the chariot, which appears in the first dumb show in *Jocasta,* the tree, used preceding Act V in *The Battle of Alcazar,* and throne, employed in the last dumb show of *A Warning for Fair Women.* Characters indigenous to both forms are the wild men in I, *Gorboduc,* the nymphs in the second dumb show in *The Misfortunes of Arthur,* such personifications as Fame in the show preceding Act V of *The Battle of Alcazar,* and the historical and legendary figures of Hercules in *Locrine,* Prologue IV, and Cyrus and Alexander in *The Scottish History of James IV,* second dumb show. The animal symbolism of the shows of genealogy is reflected in the use of the lion in *Locrine,* Prologue I.

While it is evident that themes common to both the dumb show and the street show did not have their sole source in the latter, yet the pageant contributed a great deal by first presenting certain themes in a visual medium, and establishing standard techniques for their presentation. Thus, when these themes were set forth on the stage, it was frequently in terms of such features of the pageant as tableaux, patterned movements, and symbolical characters and properties.

ALLEGORY ON PARADE

"THEY MARCH once about the stage" is as inevitable a stage direction for the legendary characters or personified abstractions of a dumb show as it is for the historical personages of a royal entry in a chronicle play. In the dumb show, as well as in the drama proper, the parades of allegorical figures seem to be related not so much to the royal entry parades as to the "mummerie." In the early manifestations of this form, the participants might be costumed as historical characters, like the Pope, emperors and cardinals who called on Richard II. Then John Lydgate in the early fifteenth century transformed the mummerie by employing allegorical characters and patterned movement in his "deuyse of a desguysing to fore the gret estates of this lande, thane being at London . . ." In the beginning of the show, the figure of Fortune enters, as the presenter recounts how this fickle goddess first favored then deserted the historical worthies Alexander and Julius Caesar, while conversely, she raised a lowly shepherd who became King Cresus. Then one by one the four virtues appear, appropriately costumed and propertied. Prudence enters with her mirror, followed by Dame Rigwysnesse with a scale, Fortitude, who bears a sword to fight against adversity, and last, Attemperaunce. After identifying and explaining each character, the expositor delivers the moral, wherein the audience is advised to follow the virtues represented by the four sisters, who will protect against the vagaries of fortune.[44]

Resembling Lydgate's "device" is the parade of the Seven Deadly Sins, with their properties and identifying speeches in Marlowe's *Faustus*. After the entering parade, each character steps forth and explains himself, very much in the manner of the pageants displaying a group of allegorical or historical figures. A similar, but more lavish procession of personified abstractions was staged by Nashe in *Summer's Last Will and*

Testament, which, as the presenter said, was a "show" and not a play. Evidently it was played before the Queen at her last stop on progress, since Summer is made to announce that she would have died before this, but that Eliza had forbidden it until her progress should have expired. In the play, the seasons with their attendant trains are called in to account for themselves, so that Summer may bequeath them fitting legacies. First summer appears, leaning on the shoulders of Autumn and Winter, and attended by a train of singing satyrs and wood nymphs. Then Ver and his followers, in suits of green moss, enter and fetch in a hobby horse and a morris dance. Next, like an old hermit, Solstitium is brought on by a number of shepherds playing recorders. Others who enter with trains and claim the succession to Summer are Sol, richly attired, with musicians before him, Orion like a hunter, Harvest carrying a scythe, accompanied by reapers with sickles, and Bacchus riding an ass trapped in ivy. Summer decides on Autumn as her heir, with Winter as overseer, and charges all of the seasons to bestow their benefits upon Elizabeth. Here the elements of the pastoral progress entertainment can be seen in the incorportation of representation, grouping, song and story in the procession of personifications.

In the splendor of its allegorical parades, *The Three Lords and Three Ladies of London* on the other hand, gives the effect of a continuous Lord Mayor's Show. First, a richly-attired lady representing London passes over the stage, two angels before and after her. The application is delivered to the audience: God guards London. From Spain, lords arrive to sue for the favor of the three ladies of London, Love, Lucre and Conscience, who will be defended by their London suitors, the lords Pomp, Policy and Pleasure. The entry of the Spanish lords, exhibiting symbolic impresses,[45] resembles the spectacular parades into the lists: Bearing a shield with the impress of a peacock, Pride is accompanied by his page Shame; Ambition enters with his device, a black horse stretching from the globe of the earth to the clouds, and is followed by his page, Treacherie; Tyrannie, whose impress is a naked child on a spear's point, is attended by his page Terror. They then act according to custom, and march once about the stage. During the procession, the expositors, a Spanish and an English herald, are busily interpreting the impresses of the lords, identifying the pages, and naming the lady to whom each lord sues. Policy explains the grouping of the Spaniards—Shame follows Pride, Treachery attends on Ambition, and Terror waits on Tyranny. Of course this play ends in the total rout of the Spanish, and a spectacular marriage procession for the triplicate heroes and heroines.

Familiar now as then is the traditional exploitation of popular devices by succeeding plays. Evidently taking note of the appeal of the allegorical procession in previous plays, *Lingua* carries the attraction to new extremes in the realm of the spectacular. Here it is not the three lords or the four seasons, but the five senses who enter in elaborate procession with an appropriate entourage. One example should suffice. In Visus' show, which he "marshalleth . . . about the stage," there marches first a page with a scutcheon bearing an eagle painted upon it; then Visus enters with a fan of peacock's feathers, and Lumen with a crown of bays and a shield with a bright sun on it. Lumen is followed by Coelum, attended by a page with a shield. Next comes a page carrying "a terrestriall Globe" before Terra, who wears "a green velvet gown stuck with branches of flowers, a crown of turrets upon her head, in her hand a key." Finally appears a herald, followed by Colour "with a rainbow out of a Cloud on her head." In pageant fashion, each member of the procession delivers an identifying speech. Light, for instance, stands forth, announces her virtues, and explains her properties:

This heavenly shield, soon as it is display'd,
Dismays the vices that abhor the light.[46]

Although *Lingua* represents the greatest elaboration of the procession of personifications, the basic pattern used by Lydgate is still present—the entry of symbolical characters who identify themselves, as in the case of the Seven Deadly Sins in *Faustus,* or are explained to the audience, as in *The Three Lords and Three Ladies of London.* Tending more and more to be presented visually are characters who were merely alluded to in earlier shows, as the victims or beneficiaries and attendants of a personification. Along with the characters, the costumes and properties have become more extensive and decorative.

TABLEAUX: FROM STREET TO STAGE

SINCE PRIMITIVE man first drew upon cave walls, the visual arts have especially manifested that sense of design which reflects man's own inherent desire for harmony and order. The popularity of the pageants was perhaps as attributable to the appeal of the intrinsic design as to the attraction of the external decoration. The total design of the *tableaux vivants,* like that of the visual arts, was immediately perceptible. Important ingredients of the pageants' total unit were, of course, the living actors employed here, as in the drama, to express a theme. The strict, formal tableaux in which these actors were arranged in the pageants reflect the mannered grouping characteristic of the art of the Middle Ages, when the street shows evolved and when the visual impression was important.

Thus the façade of a pageant arch was not unlike that of a medieval cathedral, which displayed in statuary many of the same figures who were exhibited in the pageants. So the medieval drama, its scenes little more than extended tableaux, presented a series of separate units, many dependent upon the immediate visual effect. Numerous Elizabethan plays, on the other hand, resembled more the modern drama, wherein each incident of the unfolding action contributes to the over-all unity, and the appreciation of the total design depends upon the completion of the play. Utilizing at the same time the older technique of the pageants, the Elizabethan dramatists stopped the flow of action at certain points, and created stage pictures to stress memorable and symbolical scenes.

Because of their association with actual pageants, the allegorical characters of the dumb shows or processions were natural choice for stage tableaux. In Dekker's *Old Fortunatus,* for instance, Fortune enters, accompanied by one nymph carrying the globe and another the wheel. The goddess bears chains by which she leads her victims, four kings who had been only mentioned in Lydgate's entertainment on the same theme. Treading on the kings, she ascends her throne to present to the audience the familiar tableau of Fortune surrounded by her companions and victims.

Probably *Histriomastix* represents the most consistent and effective employment of the entry and subsequent tableau grouping of the personified abstractions. In this play, Marston uses the allegorical figures and their trains not only for spectacle but also to symbolize the transition of the commonwealth from one state to the next. The visual effect of the opening scene is reminiscent of that of the pageant of Worthie Governance at Elizabeth's coronation. At the beginning of the play, Peace enters with Grammar, Logic, Rhetoric, Arithmetic, Geometry, Music and Astronomy, ascends the throne about which her companions group themselves, and then announces:

> Now sit wee high (tryumphant in our sway,)
> Encircled with the seauen-fold flower of Art,
> To tread on Barbarisme with siluer feete;[47]

Similar in theme to another pageant at Elizabeth's entry, these scenes prologue each act by depicting a flourishing and then a decayed commonwealth, together with the causes thereof. In contrast to the opening show of Peace, Pride appears at the beginning of Act III, with her companions, Vain-Glory, Hypocrisy, and Contempt. At her entry, "Pride casts a mist," and the characters occupying the stage "vanish." Surrounded by her attendants, Pride seats herself upon the throne and remarks, "Then thus . . . Pryde turns her houre and heere her Sceane beginnes." For both practical and artistic reasons, Marston varies these entries. Pride's scene ends with a banquet and a masque, after which all the players fall asleep. Then a solitary figure, Envy, appears and "breaths amongst them." She explains that she has no train, since Envy reigns alone. Bearing a close resemblance to the street shows in theme and effect, the final spectacle presents the entry of Astraea, ushered in by Fame, supported by Fortitude and Religion, and followed by Virginity and the Arts. Astraea, who is identified in a marginal notation as "Q. Eliza.", is eulogized by Peace, and then mounts her throne for the final tableau.[48]

Historical rather than allegorical figures are brought on in parade in *Macbeth* when the witches present "a show of eight Kings, [the eighth] with a glass in his hand, and Banquo last."[49] Although there has been considerable debate about the manner in which this "show" was staged, very likely the figures entered in procession one by one, since Macbeth is startled at the appearance of each additional member. On stage, the figures may have halted, in a striking depiction of a sight which had haunted Macbeth's imagination, the "line of kings," to which Banquo had been hailed as father. The group, numbering nine including Banquo, may have given the impression of a Nine Worthies Show of the ancestors of King James. As previously indicated, the membership of the Worthies' group was adaptable to the occasion, and might include the progenitors of an honored sovereign. In the procession in *Macbeth*, some of the kings are carrying properties representative of the "union of nations," a theme popular in shows celebrating James. The "twofold balls," a double representation of the globe or orb which was an insigne of sovereignity, refer to the union of England and Scotland. The "treble sceptres" may apply to England, Scotland and Ireland, whose union had been hailed in the speeches of the sybils at Oxford in 1605. Rather than passing over and off the stage, the "line of kings" might have formed a tableau upon the inner stage, while Banquo smiled, and pointed at them for his. Then the entire show might have effectively vanished with a sudden closing of the curtains of the inner stage.

While stage pictures were sometimes formed by grouping the members of the procession which had just entered, tableaux effects frequently were struck in the course of dramatic scenes. In what may be Shakespeare's earliest play, a woman is eulogized, as Elizabeth frequently was, by a comparison to the virginal Astraea, the goddess who embodied all virtues and who had reigned during the Golden Age. In 1 *Henry VI,* after the French victory at Orleans, Pucelle enters "on the walls"— the upper stage—accompanied by the Dauphin, Reignier, Alençon, and soldiers. It is the moment of glory for "France's saint," as yet untarnished by the later events of the play. Very likely a tableau was struck, similar to those mounted upon actual city gates at occasions of triumph. In his speech praising Pucelle, the Dauphin incorporates such elements of the street shows as Astraea, the garden, the pyramid, and the assurance of everlasting fame for the one honored. In addition, further well-known features of the civic celebrations are ordered—bonfires, pealing of bells, and feasting in the streets.[50]

Tableaux in the drama are always visually appealing; in addition they served both to stress a particular scene, and to represent an important political or moral theme which had been given similar presentation *en tableau* by the pageants. For striking stage pictures, both pageant and drama first chose the obvious scenes which were represented in tableau fashion in real life—the court of justice, the pagan temple, the formal trial. As discussed, *Old Fortunatus* and *Histriomastix* exemplify the theatrical effectiveness of a stage tableau displaying an enthroned personified abstraction grouped with her attendants. Londoners who admired the Temple of Janus pageant at James' entry found similar mythological characters and patterned movement in the scenes at the altar of Diana in *Pericles* and those of Mars, Venus and Diana in *The Two Noble Kinsmen*.[51] With its mounting tension placed in a framework of formal ceremony, the trial scene has held a lead in dramatic effectiveness since the ancient *Eumenides* and the medieval trial of Christ in the mystery plays and of Mankind in the moralities. Before the accused hero presents his defense in *The Arraignment of Paris,* there is a conscious grouping of the characters: "the gods being set in Dianes bower: Iuno, Pallas, Diana, Venus and Paris stand on sides before them."[52]

No one employs more effectively than does Shakespeare the short trial scene, with its combination of tableau and tension. In *The Winter's Tale,* the audience is immediately sympathetic with the accused Queen who must defend herself in the cold and formal setting of a court. A similar effect is achieved by the trial of Katherine in *Henry VIII,* where the stage directions for this scene, attributed to Shakespeare, reveal a careful attention to the arrangement of the principals:

The King takes place under the cloth of state; the two Cardinals sit under him as Judges. The Queen takes place some disance from the King. The Bishops place themselves on each side the court, in manner of a consistory; below them, the Scribes. The Lords sit next the Bishops. The rest of the Attendants stand in convenient order about the stage.

II, iv, s.d.

In *King Lear,* the tableau effect of the mock trial scene is not only striking but symbolic. At the beginning of the play, King Lear believes sovereignty is synonymous with:

> power,
> Preeminence, and all the large effects
> That troop with majesty.

> I, ii, 132 ff.

In the course of his suffering, while details of the trappings of kingship still crowd his brain, Lear comes to realize that he has given "too little care" to such fundamental issues as love for his subjects and the remedy of injustice; yet he still insists on being "every inch a king." The King finally dismisses all thought of worldly pomp, and reveals his newly-gained humility and perspective as he looks forward to the happiness of love and companionship in prison, where he and Cordelia will "laugh at gilded butterflies" and their affairs at court. Half-way through Lear's painful journey to this realization occurs an effective visual representation of the opposition of the basic values and the outward show. In a miserable hovel a trial is held. Lear has yet to learn that it is the justice, not the decor of the law court, which matters. Here, the absent forces of evil are arraigned by the forces of good—represented by the crack-brained fool, the seemingly mad Edgar and the near-insane Lear who demands the formal grouping of a court chamber:

> [To Edgar] Thou robed man of justice, take thy place.
> [To the fool] And thou, his yokefellow of equity,
>   Bench by his side.
> [To Kent] You are o'th'commission, Sit you too.

> III, vi, 38ff.

The counterpoint in *Lear* of the significant and the superficial is nowhere in the play more vividly impressed upon the audience than in this scene.

Some tableaux were neither formed by entering processions nor struck by actors in the course of the scene, but presented by a sudden, striking revelation. In the pageant displays, such an effect was achieved by draping the arch or stage upon which the tableau was mounted, and unveiling the show when the king arrived. This was done most artistically at James' entry where the silken cloud-curtains dropped at the approach of the sun-king to reveal a splendid scene. Greene effectively employs the sudden disclosure of a tableau in *A Looking Glass for London and England,* when Rasni draws the curtains of the inner stage and reveals Remilia "Stroken with thunder, blacke."[53] In a similar scene in *The Trial of Chivalry,* a sight of beauty is displayed as Burbon opens Bellamira's pavilion where she is discovered "sitting in a chayre asleepe." Affected by this tableau, he utters

> What do I see? The maiesty of heauen,
> Sit in a mayden slumber on the earth?
> What is my Bellamira turnd a goddesse . . . [54]

Later in the scene, Bellamira's face, like Remilia's beauty, is disfigured when her lover throws poison at her.

This technique of sudden disclosure became especially popular for shocking the audience by the swift revelation of a horrible sight. In *The Death of Robert Earl of Huntingdon,* it is reported that young Bruce has taken Windsor Castle, where he has found his mother and brother starved to death in a tower. He has cut a wide window therein, to display this scene, just as he discovered it, as "a spectacle to every commer by, That heaven and earth, your tyrant shame may see." The King appears at Windsor and demands that the gates be opened. Entering "uppon the walles," Bruce refuses to obey the ruler, but remarks

> . . . the gate [i.e., upper curtained space] I will,
> The gate where thy shame and my sorrow sits.

Then, pulling the cord, he announces. "See my dead mother and her famisht son." Presenting this exhibition of the King's tyranny, he dwells on the details of the gruesome spectacle, and explains that his mother's mouth is bloody, as she had bitten off her hand and offered it to the child; his teeth are unstained, as he had refused to eat it.[55]

In *Antonio's Revenge,* horror is intensified by surprise when Antonio draws the curtains which are supposed to disclose his bride and instead, "the body of Feliche, stabb'd thick with wounds, appears hung up."[56] A similar discovery takes place in *Hoffman,* where two skeletons are displayed hanging in Hoffman's cave in the inner stage. The device was still in service in 1613 when Webster employed it in the scene in which models of the bodies of her husband and children are revealed to the Duchess of Malfi.

Shakespeare uses the disclosure not for an effect of horror, but rather for one of beauty or magic. In *The Winter's Tale,* the curtains part to reveal the living statue of Hermione,[57] while Prospero in *The Tempest* suddenly presents the assembled company with a view of Miranda and Ferdinand playing chess, probably on the inner stage.[58] The employment of this striking technique in *The Tempest* seems more befitting to a magician than the realistic manner by which wizards in other plays reveal the actions of absent members.

In addition to effectively creating stage pictures, the tableaux proved useful in the presentation of scenes which, like the pageants, were symbolic of important political or moral themes. Frequently, one of the play's characters pointed out the universal application of such a scene, just as an expositor explained the themes of the pageants. Both dumb show and drama proper employed these commentators.

In *The Scottish History of James IV,* Oberon acts as presenter, standing on the upper stage and delivering the maxims implied by the dumb shows enacted below. *A Looking*

Glass for London and England, The Woman in the Moon,
and *Histriomastix* all provide characters to comment on
scenes in the main action. In *A Looking Glass for London
and England,* the prophet Oseas, brought in by an angel
and "set downe ouer the Stage in a Throne" remarks upon
the events depicted beneath and infers from them warnings
to London. For instance, after the arguing clowns leave the
stage in search of drink, Oseas announces:

> London looke on, this matter nips thee neere;
> Leaue off thy ryot, pride and symptuous cheere.
>   I, ii, 270 f.

Lyly similarly places upon the upper stage the personification
of the planet that is influencing Pandora in a particular scene
in *The Woman in the Moon.* In *Histriomastix,* personified
abstractions depicting various states of the kingdom are
grouped on the stage, while representative scenes are enacted.
In addition, Act V presents not only the stage picture, but also
a commentator upon it. *En tableau* with attendants, War
presides over the stage where ensue short incidents typical
of a warring country. At the end of the act, a scholar, mourn-
ing the rule of war and its resulting chaos, makes the moral
application:

> O, what a thing is man, that thus forgets
> The end of his creation; and each houre
> Strikes at the glory of his maker thus?[59]

As manifested in early plays, the tableau-and-commentator
device seems almost like pageant and presenter transplanted
to the stage. In *The Three Lords and Three Ladies of London,* the three ladies seat themselves on three stones, Love
on the stone of Charity, Lucre on Care, and Conscience on
Remorse. To this tableau Nemo enters, and points out a detailed application—the scalding drops which the marble of
remorse sweats are like the tears Conscience should shed in

remorse at guilt; the flint stone upon which Love is seated is as cold as the charity of the day. Just as Lucre's stone exhales cold from it and draws heat from her, so the care of Lucre has in it the force to cool the heart and draw the vital spirits. The illustration on the title page of the 1590 quarto of the play may very well depict this scene. The picture represents a tableau of seated ladies mounted pageant-wise upon a decorated arch. In the streets stands a presenter, pointing to the tableau. (See Plate VII).

While this stilted scene in Wilson's play seems consciously to be working for a pageant-like effect, other plays employ the technique more dramatically. In 1 *Tamburlaine*, for instance, Zenocrate comments upon the spectacle of the dead bodies of Bajazeth in the cage and his wife beside it:

> Those that are proud of fickle Empery
> And place their chiefest good in earthly pompe:
> Behold the Turke and his great Emperesse.
>
> V, ii, 2134 ff.

And when Remilia is disclosed stricken black in *A Looking Glass for London and England*, Oseas announces that "Pride hath his judgment."[60]

It was noted above that Shakespeare used the theme and technique of the pageant in the Temple Garden Scene with its mannered dialogue, patterned movement, symbolical properties, and political import pronounced by a commentator. A similarly stylized scene is to be found in 3 *Henry VI* where father slays son and son slays father in representation of "the ruins of civil war." The King himself acts as expositor to the symbolical, tableau-like scene:

> O piteous spectacle! O bloody times!
> Whiles lions war and battle for their dens,
> Poor harmless lambs abide their enmity.

O, pity, pity, gentle heaven, pity!
The red rose and the white are on his face,
The fatal colours of our striving houses.

. . . .

Wither one rose, and let the other flourish!
If you contend, a thousand lives must wither.

II, v, 73 ff.

To portray a political lesson, Shakespeare again employs
the stylized movement, grouping and commentator in the
depiction of Richard II's deposition, an act which, according
to sixteenth century historians, was punished by the Wars of
the Roses. Here, the mannered presentation not only em-
phasizes the symbolism of the occasion, but also enhances
the characterization. It is entirely fitting that Richard II, who
loves to stage himself to mens' eyes, recognize the scenic
value of the occasion and accordingly call for formal grouping and patterned action:

. . . . Here, cousin, seize the crown.
Here, cousin,
On this side my hand, and on that side yours.
Now is this golden crown like a deep well
That owes two buckets, filling one another,
The emptier ever dancing in the air,
The other down, unseen, and full of water.
That bucket down and full of tears am I,
Drinking my griefs whilst you mount up on high.

. . . .

Now mark me how I will undo myself.
I give this heavy weight from off my head
And this unwieldy sceptre from my hand,
The pride of kingly sway from out my heart.

IV, i, 181 ff.

Aware of the symbolical import of the scene, the Abbot comments,

A woful pageant have we here beheld.

IV, i, 321

Another self-styled actor is portrayed in *Richard III,*where the Machiavellian Richard, who has displayed his contempt for the Prince's royal entry, now stands ready to receive the "surprise" offer of the crown. Flanked by clergymen, Richard exhibits himself on the upper stage, like a tableau of the ideal prince. In the role of expositor, Buckingham explains to the crowd gathered on the main stage the significance of Richard's position between the two bishops,

Two props of virtue for a Christian prince,
To stay him from the fall of vanity;

and his properties,

And see, a book of prayer in his hand,
True ornaments to know a holy man.

III, vii, 96 ff.

Equal in irony and similar in visual effect is the welcome in *Measure for Measure,* where the entering Duke takes Angelo's hand and that of Escalus to pose between these "props of virtue." In contrast to Richard III, Henry V figures as the true ideal in a tableau effect in 2 *Henry IV*. In his first appearance as King, Henry addresses the Lord Chief Justice, and regards him as the personification of this important virtue:

Justice, ...
. . . still bear the balance and the sword;

.   .   .   .

There is my hand.
You shall be as a father to my youth;

V, ii, 102 ff.

Thus he strikes the familiar pose of the ideal king supported by a sovereign's chief virtue, Justice.

Shakespeare applied the technique of the pageant to symbolically significant scenes from classical as well as English
history. In modern productions of *Julius Caesar,* all to
often the scene of Caesar's death finds the hero falling amid
confusion. The dialogue, however, indicates that this scene
should produce a visual effect similar to a tableau depicting
the downfall of a proud and unjust king. As in the above-
mentioned incident in *Henry V,* Shakespeare is portraying
the ruler's relationship to justice, which ideally was tem-
pered with mercy. Seated in the Senate House, Caesar shows
no clemency as he sternly refuses to reconsider the banish-
ment of Metellus Cimber's brother. Before him kneels Cimber to plead for his brother; then Brutus kneels and kisses
Caesar's hand,

> I kiss thy hand, but not in flattery, Caesar . . .

and Cassius falls to Caesar's feet:

> Pardon, Caesar! Caesar, pardon!
> As low as to thy foot doth Cassius fall
> To beg enfranchisement for Publius Cimber.
>> III, i, 52 ff.

But "supple knees feed arrogance and are the proud man's
fees,"[61] for Caesar, who made his first appearance in the play
in triumph after a civil war, again exemplifies the bad ruler.
Refusing mercy to the banished man, Caesar swears that he
is not, like men of flesh and blood, "apprehensive," but
rather "Unshak'd of motion." Decius kneels too:

> Great Caesar!
> CAESAR. Doth not Brutus bootless kneel?
>> III, i, 67 ff.

At this point, Casca, who stands behind Caesar, stabs the
proud, unmerciful man. Having gained the sympathy of the
audience for the dead Caesar, Antony describes the incident
in a different light, but he remembers the tableau:

You show'd your teeth like apes, and fawn'd like
   hounds,
And bow'd like bondmen, kissing Caesar's feet;
Whilst damned Casca, like a cur, behind
Struck Caesar on the neck.

V, i, 41 ff.

The dumb shows, parades of personified abstractions, and tableau effects were not among the innovations in Elizabethan drama. Rather, they looked back to medieval, semi-dramatic forms, such as the mummerie and the pageant. The vigor of the Elizabethan drama may well be due in part to this blending of the traditional with the experimental. Especially in the case of Shakespeare, the skillfully-incorporated older devices harmonize perfectly with the total effect, while at the same time they enrich a particular scene with overtones of the universality and splendor of the original form.

OVID AMONG THE GOATS

WHEN SUMMER came, Elizabeth combined politics with pleasure, and journeyed through her realm to visit towns, universities, and noblemen's estates. The royal procession brought color and excitement to the country roads, peopled by travelers on horse or foot, yeomen with their rude carts and occasionally an aristocrat in a carriage. Elizabeth's entourage included lavishly attired courtiers riding horseback and attending the sovereign who sat resplendent in a canopied litter. In the rear, wound hundreds of wagons of provisions, necessary if undecorative. Thus Elizabeth brought to her subjects throughout the land the living image of a splendid and gracious sovereign. At the same time, the court was maintained and entertained largely at the expense of the noblemen whose estates the Queen honored by her royal residence. (Cf. Plate IX).

In their receptions, the towns imitated the London pageants of good government and flourishing trade. On the country estates, there developed a form of entertainment which employed many of the street shows' legends, figures and properties with a view to pleasing and diverting the ruler by eulogizing her private virtues, rather than by exemplifying her public ones. From the moment of her entrance into the estate until her exit, Elizabeth with her attendant train moved in an Arcadia where nymphs sang welcome songs, shepherds and foresters (appropriately attired) wooed shepherdesses, sybils prophesied a happy reign, fairies danced in rings, and well-known characters from mythology and legend flocked to offer homage to the sovereign of surpassing beauty and virtue. There were love-debates and singing contests by day, masques and fireworks by night. At the sight of the virgin queen, wild men grew tame. Music and verse pervaded the atmosphere. In a pastoral setting transformed by Ovidian devices of enchantment and myth, Diana hailed the royal votress of her order and assisted her at the hunt. Story tellers attired as pilgrims of love or hermits pointed to trees or bushes and recounted the metamorphoses of lovers into landscape. As the Queen walked about the grounds, across her path might dart a satyr-pursued nymph, to take refuge in a tree which would later "rive" to permit her to emerge and tell her tale. Or a romance was partly narrated, partly performed, with the denouement invariably involving the fulfillment of a prophecy concerning the arrival of a nonpareil ruler. Instead of the formal ceremonies of the town, playlets were designed especially to lead to the presentation of gifts more decorative and original than those of the city. Masques and shows accompanied feasts where the food itself was molded into, or trimmed with, fantastic shapes of birds, animals, and other figures. At Elizabeth's departure, the estate was draped in black, while mournful music sounded and black-clad actors—nymphs, sybils, shepherds, foresters—stood weeping and sadly waving farewell. All of the music, dancing, allegory, poetry, and decoration of the entertainments was attuned to the dual strain of love and beauty: ennobling love demonstrated by service to the queenly paragon of virtue and beauty.

In the mechanics of presentation, the entertainments extended the historical, mythological, and legendary material which the street shows could represent only with limited action and dialogue. The estate entertainments tended not merely to display such characters as gods, goddesses and personified abstractions, but to present them over a period of several days, in portrayal of the legends with which they were associated. Perhaps a lake on the estate, plus the popularity of the Arthurian element in entertainments determined the theme of the shows at Kenilworth. As Elizabeth crossed the bridge, she was greeted by the Lady of the Lake, who recounted her history subsequent to the dissolution of the Round Table. Surrounded by an aquatic entourage, the Lady related that during the troubled times in England after Arthur's death, she had taken refuge on the estate of Kenilworth, and emerged only now that this third visit of Elizabeth assured peace. On the following day, the Queen was walking about the estate when Triton approached, to inform her that the Lady of the Lake was besieged by Sir Bruce, a cousin revenging Merlin, whom the Lady had enclosed in a rock. According to Merlin's prophecy, she could be freed from Bruce's assault only by a maid superior even to the Lady of the Lake—Elizabeth, of course.

A regular practice at royal entertainments, this expansion and adaptation of legend to compliment the Queen is well

illustrated by the evolution of the Judgment of Paris as a subject for celebration of the sovereign. Leland reports that at
the entry of Margaret to Edinburgh in 1503 on the occasion
of her marriage to James IV of Scotland, a show mounted on
a scaffold presented Paris, the three goddesses, and Mercury,
who gave the golden apple to Paris, who in turn delivered it
to Venus, the fairest. The same group was displayed at the
Little Conduit in Cheapside, in 1533, when Anne went
through the streets in procession from the Tower to Westminster where she was to be crowned Queen. Paris was about to
bestow the golden apple on Venus, but at the arrival of Anne,
it was decided that she embodied the combined virtues of
the three goddesses. However, the golden ball was too lowly
a gift for the Queen; the crown was the only fitting reward
for her worthiness. The sentiment continued in the reign
of Anne's famous daughter, of whom Gascoigne in his "Vanities of Beauty" declared:

> This Queen it is, who (had she satt in feeld
> When Paris judged, that Venus bare the bell,)
> The prize were hers, for she deserves it well.[62]

Towards the end of Elizabeth's reign, in the "Triumphs of
Oriana," George Kirbye similarly celebrated her:

> Her apple Venus yields as best befitting
> A Queen beloved most dearly.[63]

This same adjustment of the story is revealed in a play
designed for the private, courtly audience—Peele's *Arraignment of Paris*. After the method of the progress entertainment, the fable here is expanded to incorporate welcoming
ceremonies, songs, the "shows" which the goddesses present,
incidental views of shepherds and shepherdesses, and finally
the ensemble scene and presentation of the apple to Elizabeth.

When the play opens, it is learned that the three goddesses, Juno, Pallas and Venus are coming on progress to Diana's
bower. Flora's welcoming devices are flower likenesses of
the distinguished visitors;[64] Pomona, Fauna, and Pan greet
the goddesses with songs and gifts. Also present in the play
are the inevitable references to Ovid's *Metamorphoses,* which
seemed to be the favorite reading matter of the devisers of
progress entertainments. As did many a character attired as
a hermit or pilgrim on the estates, Oenone and Paris list tales
of metamorphosed lovers, among the thirteen different "fab-
ula" which they discuss, while in Act II, Juno narrates the
myth of Echo. In addition, the three shows which the goddesses present are typical of progress entertainments: a tree
of gold laden with golden crowns and diadems, a march of
nine of Pallas' knights in armor, and the appearance of Helen
of Troy, lavishly dressed, accompanied by four cupids. Another feature of the progress shows may be reflected in the
Colin interlude, with its background in the eclogue and
casual insertion in the main story. (Similarly regarded as a
separate show is the wooing scene in *As You Like It,* wherein
the old shepherd Corin, having invited Rosalind and Celia
to "see a pageant truly play'd," exhibits Silvius courting
Phebe.[65]) Vulcan's pursuit of one of Diana's nymphs in
Peele's play is reminiscent of such progress entertainments
as Apollo's chase after Daphne, staged at Sudley. At Paris'
trial, the actors are arranged *en tableau,* just as they are in
the concluding scene. In the latter, all the principals are
grouped on stage, as the Fates enter and surrender to Elizabeth their powers and instruments—the distaff of Clotho,
Lachesis' spindle and thread, and Atropos' knife. Finally,
Diana approaches the most distinguished member of the
audience, Elizabeth, and presents the golden ball to the Queen
who possesses the combined wisdom, state and beauty of the
three disputing goddesses.

To please the courtly audience for which they were designed, plays other than *The Arraignment of Paris* borrowed characteristic devices from the progress entertainments. Like Peele's play, concerned with a progress visit, *Love's Labour's Lost* holds a special appeal for an audience which would recognize in it the features which made Elizabeth's own sojourns at the estates so memorable. Thus the Princess and her ladies—here because of the exigencies of the plot—reside in a separate structure on the grounds, although it is not as spacious as the Queen's temporary hall of state constructed at Elvetham. The outer walls of the latter "were all covered with boughs, and clusters of ripe hasell nuttes, the insides with arras, the roofe of the place with workes of ivy leaves."[66] The short, complimentary lyrics and sonnets, in varying degrees of excellence, flourished at the progress entertainments. *Love's Labour's Lost* is no exception. Here, some of the laudatory verses may even have been directed at Elizabeth herself—the poem addressed to the "queen of queens,"[67] for example. All too numerous are the progress prototypes of Holofernes' verse which commemorates a minutia of the Princess' pastime, the killing of the "pretty pleasing pricket."[68] The hunt, of course, was a favorite diversion of Elizabeth on progress visits. Just as they did at Warwick, Cowdray, Althorp, and Kenilworth, the country people come to the estate to present some entertainment before the visiting royalty in *Love's Labour's Lost*. As was frequently the case in real life, this show is planned by the pedantic schoolmaster. O. J. Campbell, who first noted the resemblance between *Love's Labour's Lost* and the progress entertainments, has pointed out that the unusual ending of the play, in which "Jack hath not Gill," reflects the actual circumstances, where casual flirtations terminated with the visit.[69]

The entertainments on the estates elaborated upon the civic water shows in the same manner as they expanded the techniques of the city pageants. If a pond, like the one at Kenilworth, was lacking, an artificial one was built, as was the case at Elvetham. More warlike than the Kenilworth show of the Lady of the Lake, the Elvetham water pageantry in 1591 reflected the predilection for the sea siege. The allegorical show centered about three main properties—the Armada as a snail mount, a monster with horns of wild fire; a Fort sent by Neptune for Elizabeth's defense; and a Ship Isle whose mast turned to trees, receiving life from the "verdure" of Elizabeth's looks. Fireworks lit the air, sea gods sang songs and delivered fanciful presents; the water gods skirmished with Sylvanus and his foresters.[70]

Scholars have previously conjectured that the following passage in *A Midsummer Night's Dream,* which contains elements of the progress shows, may refer to this entertainment at Elvetham:[71]

> Thou rememb'rest
> Since once I sat upon a promontory
> And heard a mermaid, on a dolphin's back,
> Uttering such dulcet, and harmonious breath
> That the rude sea grew civil at her song,
> And certain stars shot madly from their spheres
> To hear the sea-maid's music . . . .
> That very time I saw (but thou couldst not)
> Flying between the cold moon and the earth
> Cupid, all arm'd. A certain aim he took
> At a fair Vestal, throned by the West,
> And loos'd his love-shaft smartly from his bow,
> As it should pierce a hundred thousand hearts.
> But I might see young Cupid's fiery shaft
> Quench'd in the chaste beams of the wat'ry moon,
> And the imperial vot'ress passed on,
> In maiden meditation, fancy-free.
>
> II, i, 148 ff.

"Throned by the West" reflects the Queen's customary station at these outdoor shows, where it was necessary to keep the sun out of the royal eyes. In addition, it is interesting to note the prominence of the word "West" in relation to the Queen's position in the illustration to the twice-issued quarto which reported the Elvetham entertainment. (See Plate VIII).

Besides the fireworks and the sea show, additional elements of the entertainment at Elvetham seem to be reflected in *A Midsummer Night's Dream*. For instance, one of the features of the entertainment was a dance of fairies and their Queen, Aureola, who announced that she was the wife of Auberon, the Fairy King. Played by the small, talented boys of Elizabeth's choir, the fairies at the entertainment sang songs written in the same octo-syllabic couplets as were the lyrics of the fairies in Shakespeare's play:

> Elisa is the fairest Quene
> That ever trod upon this greene,[72]

they sang at Elvetham, and in *A Midsummer Night's Dream*:

> And I serve the Fairy Queen,
> To dew her orbs upon the green.
>
> II, i, 8f.

Preceding Oberon's long speech just quoted, Titania tells how "in the spiced Indian air," she and the changeling boy's mother had

> . . . laugh'd to see the sails conceive
> And grow big-bellied with the wanton wind;

which the vot'ress

> Would imitate, and sail upon the land
> To fetch me trifles, and return again,
> As from a voyage, rich with merchandise.
>
> II, i, 124ff.

In the Elvetham water show, gold-breasted India, who accompanies Nereus, sends as a gift to Elizabeth the ship whose swollen sails can be seen in the illustration.

On the third morning of the Queen's stay at Elvetham, musicians disguised in country attire came to sing under her window a song of Coridon and Phyllida. Although, to be sure, the names of the shepherd and his lass are common ones in the pastoral, some connection may exist between the above-mentioned song and the Fairy Queen's accusation of Oberon:

> When thou hast stolen away from fairyland,
> And in the shape of Corin sat all day,
> Playing on pipes of corn, and versing love
> To amorous Phillida.

II, i, 65 ff.

It is notable that all of these seeming-reflections of the Elvetham entertainment occur in the first scene of the second act.

Like the progress shows, *A Midsummer Night's Dream* incorporates elements from Ovid's *Metamorphoses*. There is, greatly extended, the chase through the forest, during the course of which Helena likens her pursuit of Demetrius to a reversal of the Apollo-Daphne story.[73] Also, the *Metamorphoses* seems to have suggested the entertainments proferred to Theseus—the battle with the centaurs, and the riot of the tipsy bacchanals, which he refuses in favor of a dramatization of another Ovidian myth. Although the delicate legend of Pyramus and Thisbe may be most inappropriate for Bottom and his crew to present, they at least choose their subject from the most popular source for such shows.

Especially adaptable to outdoor presentation were these favorite myths from the *Metamorphoses,* whose characters inhabited just such a pastoral never-never land as the progress entertainment sought to create. The imaginative and the

practical aspects were both served. Requiring little preparation and less expense, a pleasing diversion could be built
around an appropriately costumed character who would
point out that certain natural shrubs and trees on the estate
were metamorphosed lovers, whose stories he recounted. He
might or might not be supported by an enactment of the
legend. Such a technique was used at Kenilworth by George
Gascoigne who, attired as Sylvanus, told the story of Zabeta,
a beautiful nymph of Diana whose rejections had resulted
in the metamorphoses of her suitors. In a "strange and cruel
metamorphosis," Constance had become an oak, as unmov-
able as ever against the blasts of nature. Inconstancie had
been changed into a poplar, "whose leaves move and shake
with the least breathe or blast," Vainglory had turned into
an ash tree, "that busie elfe Contention," into a nearby bram-
ble briar, and Ambition was appropriately transformed into
a branch of Ivy. Zabeta's most persistent suitor, Deepdesire,
had become a holly bush, "furnished on every side with sharpe
pricking leaves, to prove the restlesse prickes of his privie
thoughts." Suddenly the bush shook, and in behalf of the
pastoral gods, Deepdesire implored the Queen to remain
longer on the estate. A lament mourned the departure of
Dame Pleasure:

> Farewell sweet, for whom I taste such sower;
> Farewell delight, for whom I dwell in dole;
> Free will, farewell, farewell my fancies flower,
> Farewell content, whom cruell cares controle.[74]

On the same progress, the Queen visited Woodstock, where
she was entertained one day by a sad song coming from an
oak tree, into which a lover had been metamorphosed; at
Sudley, she watched a portrayal of Apollo's pursuit of Daphne.
In *Edward II,* Gaveston plans a typical progress entertainment for the King—a depiction of the metamorphosis of

Actaeon, complete with dancing satyrs, and nymphs portrayed by boy actors:

> And in the day, when he shall walke abroad,
> Like Syluan Nimphes my pages shall be clad,
> My men like Satyres grazing on the lawnes,
> Shall with their Goate feete daunce an antick hay.
> Sometime a louelie boye in Dians shape,
> With haire that gilds the water as it glides,
> Crownets of pearle about his naked armes,
> And in his sportfull hands an Oliue tree,
> To hide those parts which men delight to see,
> Shall bathe him in a spring, and there hard by,
> One like Actaeon peeping through the groue,
> Shall by the angrie goddesse be transformde.
>
> 11. 57 ff.

In *Love's Metamorphosis, Midas* and *Endymion,* Lyly consciously employs features of Ovid's *Metamorphoses* which were popular with his select audience. Like the progress entertainment writers, Lyly also uses pastoral and myth for the allegory of court affairs, a subject of special appeal to the audience of the private theatre. By its very insistence that it is a fantasy to which "we hope in our times none will apply pastimes," the prologue of *Endymion* seems to invite interpretation as a court allegory, as do the myths performed at the progress entertainments. In the pamphlet detailing the entertainment at Woodstock, the author calls attention to the "audacity" of the hermit's tale,

in which tale if you marke the woords with this present world, or were acquainted with the state of the deuises, you shoulde finde no lesse hidden then uttered, and no lesse uttered then shoulde deserue a double reading ouer, euen of those (with whom I finde you a companion) that haue disposed their houres to the study of great matters.[75]

The Metamorphoses had long been a source of allegory.

Plate V. "Truth the Daughter of Time," pageant theme at Elizabeth's entry and emblem in Geoffrey Whitney, *Choice of Emblemes,* 1586.

Plate VI (below). The triumphal arch "with sodaine falling broken all to dust." *A Theatre for Worldlings,* 1569.

The pleasant and Stately
Morall, of the three Lordes
and three Ladies of London.

With the great Ioy and Pompe, Solempnized at their Mariages: Commically interlaced with much honest Mirth, for pleasure and recreation, among many Morall obseruations and other important matters of due Regard. by R. W.

LONDON.

Printed by R. Ihones, at the Rose
and Crowne neere Holburne Bridge, 1590.

Plate VII. Arch, expositor and pageant, probably depicting a scene from *The Three Lords and Three Ladies of London*, title page, 1590.

In the medieval tradition, Arthur Golding's preface to his translation of the tales in 1565 pointed out their symbolical significance. Phaeton, for example, represented "the nature of blind ambition," while Daphne was "the mirror of Chastity." These pagan deities were not to be considered as gods, said Golding, but as symbols of "some further thing and purposes by those devises ment."[76] While Golding depicted the Ovidian figures as being representative of a moral allegory, the street shows and progress entertainments used these characters from myth and those from legend for political allegory, as well. In the public entertainments, Arthur had long signified the ideal Tudor king and Truth or Astraea, Elizabeth, when they appeared in a work which made extensive use of the political allegory of characters from myth, morality and legend, *The Faerie Queene*.

Like Lyly's *Endymion, Midas,* and *Sappho and Phao, Cynthia's Revels* employs the progress entertainments' pastoral and mythological characters to present a court allegory, since Jonson found this method most effective for presenting satire to the ladies and gentlemen of the court.[77] At the beginning of the play, Diana proclaims solemn revels which she will attend in the hope of defeating the slanders which have been perpetrated against her because of her "divine justice" rendered to Actaeon. She decrees that when the revels are held, it will be lawful for all manner of persons to visit her palace, court her nymphs, and present shows. The cast of characters reveals the same infinite variety which peopled the progress entertainments: Echo, Mercury, Amorphus, and the women and men of the court all partake in the celebrations. The courtiers, who are manifestations of vices, present a show in which they masquerade as virtues. Cupid in the guise of Anteros introduces the masque of the women of the court disguised as virgins from Queen Perfection, and the men of the court attired as the four cardinal properties.

All of them bear devices which are explained after the manner of the allegorical procession. Cynthia, however, is undeceived, and causes the sinful courtiers to be unmasked, exposed, and punished.

An interesting real-life parallel to this incident is to be found in the presentation of an actual masque in the same year as Jonson's play, at the celebration of the marriage of Lord Herbert and Anne Russell. Eight lady maskers entered as muses dancing to Apollo's music and chose eight other ladies to dance with them. "Mrs. Fetton went to the queen and woed her to dawnce. Her Majesty asked what she was? *Affection,* she said. *Affection,* said the Queen, is false. Yet her majestie rose and dawnced."[78]

Much of the allegory of the progress entertainments was concerned with special suits of the host to the Queen, as demonstrated by the show of Zabeta at Kenilworth. George Gascoigne, who devised the show for Leicester, reported that it "never came to execution, the cause whereof I cannot attribute to any other thing than to lack of opportunity and seasonable weather." It is most likely that the play was too outspoken an attempt to demonstrate to the Queen the desirability of marriage. In the show, as mentioned above, the nymph Zabeta is implored by Iris to follow Juno, the goddess of chastity. The play closes with a long speech by Iris on the joys and advantages of marriage, concluding

Yet never wight felt perfect bliss, but such as wedded bene.[79]

Whether or not the entertainment involved a specific suit on the part of the host, all the devices were intended to have personal relevance to the sovereign. Frequently, the theme was one of unselfish devotion to the ruler on the part of such Endymion-like subjects as Loricus at Woodstock and Quarrendon.[80] As mentioned above, Elizabeth's own limited participation was responsible for a type of welcoming ceremony which involved an instantaneous change wrought on an uncivilized character by the mere appearance of the Queen. This was not an exclusive feature of the welcome, but might be effectively employed at any time during the sovereign's stay at the estate. As Elizabeth hunted at Kenilworth one day, a savage man dressed in ivy bounded out of the woods to confront her and her hunting party, but stricken by the appearance of the Queen, was immediately humbled, for

> . . . no man can be so base
> But needs must mount, if once it see
> A sparke of perfect grace.[81]

In *Every Man Out of His Humour*, Jonson employs this device to bring about the reform of Macilente, who is cured of his humour of Envy by the sight of Queen Elizabeth, at which he exclaims:

> . . . in her graces
> All my malicious powers have lost their stings.
> Enuie is fled my soule, at the sight of her . . .
> . . . .
> So, in the ample, and vnmeasur'd floud
> Of her perfections, are my passions drown'd:
> And I haue now a spirit as sweet, and cleere,
> As the most rarifi'd and subtile aire.[82]

Under criticism, Jonson revised this denouement, but included it in the quarto, with the following preface: "It had another *Catastrophe* or Conclusion, at the first playing: which . . . many seem'd not to rellish it; and therefore 'twas since alter'd." He went on to defend the original version as follows:

1. There hath been *President* of the like Presentation in diuers Playes: and is yeerely in our Cittie *Pageants* or shewes of *Triumph*.

2. . . . *Macilente* being so strongly possest with Enuie . . . no . . . common *Obiect* . . . shoulde effect so suddaine and straunge a cure vpon him, as the putting him cleane *Out of his Humour*.

After two more points, he concluded that the best way to express the power of the Queen's virtues was to depict the working of a miracle on such a person as Macilente, who had come to court to malign, but "sodainly . . . the verie wonder of her *Presence* strikes him to the earth dumbe, and astonisht."[83]

Jonson here indicates that the device was popular in city pageants as well as in progress entertainments. It will be recalled that his own show at James' entry depicted the dispersal of the clouds at the entry of the "sun" King. This technique, wherein a sudden change is brought about by the appearance of a virtuous character, was effective in presenting personified abstractions in conflict. It demonstrated the dramatic defeat of evil by good which needed no action nor weapon other than virtue. At the end of *Histriomastix*, Poverty and her attendants vanish at the approach of Peace, and in a pageant in Dekker's Lord Mayor's Show for 1612, Envy is conquered by the bright beams of Virtue.

Thus the Queen served as the *deus ex machina* of many a progress show, even though her participation was limited to deciding a debate, as required by Sidney's show at Wanstead, naming a ship as she did at Elvetham, or merely appearing on the scene. Her royal presence proved the solution to innumerable complicated romances, narrated and enacted, which involved prophecies dependent upon the arrival of the paragon of virtue, beauty and sovereignty. Like those in Sidney's *Arcadia*, *The Winter's Tale*, and *Cymbeline*, the prophecies seemed as impossible as they were intricate. At Woodstock in 1575, the devoted Hemetes had been stricken blind by Venus, never to recover unless two of the most valiant knights should fight, two of the most constant lovers meet, and the most virtuous lady in the world be there to look on, all at one time, in one place, in a country of most peace. Elizabeth arrived just in time.

AMATEUR SHOWS

Undaunted by the professional city pageants and sumptuous estate entertainments, the Queen's subjects proferred their amateur offerings to her, and their "tongue-tied simplicity" was courteously received.

> The more and less came in with cap and knee;
> Met him in boroughs, cities, villages,
> Attended him on bridges, stood in lanes,
> Laid gifts before him, proferr'd him their oaths . . .
> IV, iii, 68 ff.

says Hotspur, describing Bolingbroke's popularity in 1 *Henry IV,* in a passage which might well be applied to Elizabeth's own progresses.

As the Queen's procession made its way through city streets and country roads, the indefatigable Elizabeth seemed always to have responded graciously to the many impromptu tributes and greetings offered by her demonstrative subjects. The pamphlet report of her coronation remarked of her behavior on this occasion:

. . . in all her passage, she did not only shew her most gracious love toward the people in generall, but also privately, if the baser personages had offered her Grace any flowers or such like as a signification of their good wyll, or moved to her any sute, she most gently . . . staid her chariot and heard theyr requestes.[84]

King James was less responsive to such amateur offerings. At his coronation celebration there stood, on a corner,

> . . . an old man with a white beard, of the age of three-score and nineteen, who had seene the change of Four Kings and Queenes, and now beheld the Triumphs of the Fifth, which by his report exceeded all the reste; wherefore as hopeful never to behold the like, yet he would of his own accord, doe the which should shew his duty and old love, that was to speak a fue lines, that his sonne had made him, which lines were to this purpose, he himself attired in greene.

The aged citizen had intended to recite to the King an eighteen-line verse of salutation and blessing, but the "preasing multitude so overshadowed him. . . that the King past by."[85]

The old man's situation is almost singular in its pathos; the apparent humorous aspect of most of the amateur presentations in city and country was appreciated by the playwrights. Published in 1594, the quarto of the anonymous *A Knack to Know a Knave* advertised in its subtitle the most popular scene in the play: "Kemps applauded Merrimentes of the men of Goteham, in receiuing the King into Goteham." A similar appeal was to be found in the demonstrations of Turnop and his crew in *John a Kent and John a Cumber*.

Likewise, Shakespeare in *The Taming of the Shrew* alludes to the ludicrous visual effect of some of the amateurish shows presented for the Queen. When Lucentio and Tranio arrive at Padua, they spy a strange procession approaching: the fussy Baptista, followed by his daughters Katherina and Bianca, and the suitors Hortensio and the doddering Gremio. "Lucentio, Tranio stand by," as Lucentio asks, "What company is this?" to which his grinning servant replies, "Master, some show to welcome us to town."[86]

In *2 Henry IV*, preceding the entry of the King's coronation procession, Falstaff comes on with his companions, Shallow,

Pistol, Bardolph and the boy, and groups his friends about
him as if arranging a show to greet the new King:

> Stand here by me, Master Robert Shallow . . . .
> Come here, Pistol, stand behind me!
>
> V, v, 5 ff.

Then the fat knight regrets the lack of new liveries, a requisite for coronations,[87] but decides that "this poor show
doth better." Acting as his own expositor, he goes on to explain the theme of his "show," a well-worn one:

> this doth infer the zeal I had to see him . . . . It shows my
> earnestness of affection. . . . My devotion. . . . to stand stained
> with travel and sweating with desire to see him . . .
>
> V, v, 14 ff.

So that the portly and perspiring Falstaff strikes his pose,
flanked by bonfire-nosed Bardolph and Shallow, a veritable
Father Time, and backed by Pistol, who supplies the inevitable Latin motto, conveniently translated into English:

> 'Tis 'semper idem,' for 'absque hoc nihil est.'
> 'Tis all in every part.
>
> V, v, 30 f.

Critics have long puzzled over the application of these
Latin quotations. If Shakespeare was actually intending a
tableau-like burlesque "show of Zeal," the use of such mottoes
in Latin, with English translations, would drive home to
the audience the intended effect. "Semper idem," the Queen's
own heraldic device, had long been prominent in processions, and served as the theme of a show presented before
Elizabeth at Quarrendon in 1592. "Absque hoc nihil est,"
which may very well be receiving the customarily inept
translation into " 'tis all in every part," might be intended
also as a humorous *applicatio*: the leering Falstaff represents
a loyal subject's most important duty, zeal,[88] which in England

"is all in every part," that is, both constant and widespread, as how better displayed than by the corpulent Sir John? Another prevalent theme of the pageants, the new King's fame, is hailed by Pistol.[89] Later, Fluellen in *Henry V* compares Henry's own conduct in this incident to that of one of the Nine Worthies, Alexander the Great.[90]

Another interpretation of the Latin quotations might be considered. When Pistol remarks that without this there is nothing, " 'Tis all in every part," he may be praising the "show's" consistency, a primary requirement of such devices, according to Ben Jonson. In defending his denouement in *Every Man Out of his Humour*, Jonson had appealed to the precedent set by the pageant, a form which he felt should maintain as did the drama, certain standards of art. Perhaps his precepts concerning the pageant had sounded through the Mermaid Tavern or the Globe tiring house before they were published with . . . *King James his Royall and Magnificient Entertainement through his Honorable Cittie of London* . . . where Jonson states:

. . . the nature and propertie of these Deuices being, to present alwaies some one entire bodie, or figure, consisting of distinct members, and each of those expressing it selfe in the own actiue spheare, yet all, with that generall harmonie so connexed, and disposed, as no one little part can be missing to the illustration of the whole: where also is to be noted, that the Symboles vsed, are not, neither ought to be, simply Hieroglyphickes, Emblemes, or Impreses, but a mixed character, partaking somewhat of all, and perculiarly apted to these more magnificent Inuentions: wherein, the garments and ensignes deliuer the nature of the person, and the word the present office. Neither was it becomming, or could it stand with the dignitie of these shewes (after the most miserable and desperate shift of the Puppits) to require a Truch man, or (with the ignorant Painter) one to write, *This is a Dog;* or *This is a Hare*: but so to be presented, as vpon the view, they might, without cloud or obscuritie, declare themselues to the sharpe and learned . . .[91]

In towns visited on progress, the amateur aspect of the welcome and the pageants was more manifest than in London, where, aside from spontaneous gestures from the people, the devices were planned by professional writers like Peele and Jonson. On the estates, there developed the custom of inviting the country people to offer to the visiting sovereign such entertainments as these rustics might devise, usually with the help of the local schoolmaster. Along with the stately measures of the Lady of the Lake show and the Latin verses from the gods at Kenilworth, a rural "Bryde-ale" was presented, preceded by a country version of the courtly joust. As "the lusty lads and bold bachelors of the parish" paraded into the tilt yard, foremost among them was the future bridegroom; like any serious courtly contender he bore appropriate devices, as described by Robert Laneham:

a pair of harvest glovez on his hands, az a sign of good husbandry: a pen and inkhorn at his bak; for he woold be knowen to be bookish . . . . well beloved yet of his mother, that lent him a nu mufflar for a napkin that was tyed to hiz girdl for lozyng.[92]

A less elaborate but more popular amateur entertainment was the country dance. At Warwick in 1572, her rural subjects came to dance in the court of the castle, while the Queen watched from a window, and a similar dance was presented at Cowdray. Examples of the country dance in drama are numerous. Heywood effectively employs the device in *A Woman Killed with Kindness,* which ends on a somber note, after beginning with the liveliness of a country dance celebrating the wedding of John Frankford and Anne. Sometimes the sovereign was entertained by that favorite form of folk dance, the morris,[93] as at Althorp in 1603. In *The Two Noble*

Kinsmen, "the dainty domine, the schoolmaster," who "does all, ye know," presents the morris dancers: "four Countrymen and Bavian, Wenches, with a Tabourer," who waylay the hunting Duke and his company in the woods to perform before them.[94]

At the sheep-shearing festival in *The Winter's Tale,* "a dance of Shepherds and Shepherdesses" entertains the noble visitor, who is none other than the disguised King himself. Attired as Flora, Perdita, like the actual goddess in *The Arraignment of Paris,* has welcomed the royal guest and presented him with flowers. After the shepherds and shepherdesses bow out, another dance is announced. Twelve satyrs—three carters, three shepherds, three neatherds, and three swineherds—have come to perform before the visitor. Feeling that his guest may have been tired by the festivities, the shepherd remarks:

Away! We'll none on't. Here has been too much homely foolery already. I know, sir, we weary you.

But Polixenes, in the tradition of the gracious ruler, replies:

You weary those that refresh us. Pray let's see these four threes of herdsmen.

IV, iv, 340 ff.

This incident combines such features of the progress entertainment[95] as the welcome, pastoral figures, and country dance, as well as a patterned love-scene, resembling the "pageant truly play'd" between Phebe and Silvius in *As You Like It.* Before an audience consisting of the Shepherd, Polixenes and Camillo, Perdita and Florizel make declarations of love which are commented upon by the onlookers. The formal, almost exhibition-like interlude is about to culminate in a betrothal when it is abruptly interrupted by Polixenes' angry revelation of his true identity.[96]

Very likely, Elizabeth sometimes halted the progress to witness graciously such a country celebration as the sheep-shearing in *The Winter's Tale,* but most often, the country folk brought their dances or shows to the estate which the Queen was visiting. At progress time upon the estates, along with the courtiers, the noblemen-hosts, the hired actors, and writers, were to be found these local inhabitants, gaping at the shows and awaiting their turn to perform. They probably provided much of the incidental comedy. During the show at Elvetham, "Sylvanus, being so ugly, and running toward the bower to the end of the Pound, affrighted a number of the countrey people, that they ran from him for feare, and thereby moved great laughter."[97] Such low-comedy figures might be loosely incorporated into the courtly-pastoral set-ting of *Endymion* to produce an effect of realism rather than of incongruity. However, these same seemingly dispar-ate elements are more happily combined in *A Midsummer Night's Dream,* where the Duke, Hippolyta, and their court, the fairies, and Bottom and his tradesmen all wander with ease through the outdoor setting, just as such diverse figures did on the estates. During the interval between these two plays, a method more unified than Lyly's had been discovered for introducing humor into plays which contained elements of the progress entertainments.

Actually, as Laneham describes the Kenilworth country "Bryde-ale" and run at quintain, the rustic entertainment must have been received by the sophisticated courtier in much the same manner as a patron of the professional theatre today would view the offering of a group of local amateurs. Into a drama containing features of the progress entertain-ment, therefore, could be introduced a humorous subplot concerned with the preparation and presentation of a show by country or town amateurs. It might employ such devices as a farcical rehearsal, the pompous pedant, and the final presentation of a show which, like its real-life counterparts, abounded in bad poetry and dealt with a stock theme delivered by clumsy oafs, to the amusement of the courtiers— but with the indulgence of the ruler.

Among the first to use such a subplot is pageanteer-playwright Anthony Munday, in *John a Kent and John a Cumber*, produced about 1594. To celebrate the arrival of Pembroke, Turnop and "his crew of clownes &· a Minstrell" prepare a show amid quarrels and horseplay in which Turnop, like Bottom, contends for the biggest role. Finally, the show is presented, following nervous, last-minute promptings from Turnop: "Thomas, firk it with your fiddle, Spurling, you play the Moore, vaunce vp your Tun, and Robert, holde your porrenger right, least you spill the conceit, for heere they come:"

Enter Pembrook, Moorton, Oswen, Amery, to them this crew marching, one drest lik a Moore, with a Tun painted with yellow oker, another with a Porrenger full of water an[a pen in it, Turnop speaketh the Oration.   11. 365 ff.

Explaining the extremely literal devices, Turnop calls attention to his own artistic contribution:

> . . . . first the golden Tunne,
> borne by that monstrous Murrian black a Moore,
> Mortonus Earlus in thy prayse is doone.
> This shining brook hemd in with this fierce shoare
> That hath [
> is peerelesse Penbrooke, if I roue not [w]yd[e
> As for the two last rymes, right woorshipfull, [an] d m[
> wise, by the error of the Authour ouerslipped, is th[
> mothie Turnop the Oratour newly corrected, to wit[
> This princely pen vp prauncing by the sydes,
> And so we wishe ye bothe two blessed brydes.
>   11. 378 ff.

The next morning, just as Elizabeth was awakened at Elvetham by fairies and minstrels who sang under her window, so heroines Marian and Sydanen are serenaded by a song prepared by the largess-inspired Turnop. The music arouses instead the future bridegrooms, who discover that their brides-to-be have fled. Thus, the amateur entertainment here becomes integrated with the plot itself.

John a Kent and John a Cumber are also busy devising shows to entertain the notables. John a Cumber presents a mysterious "antique" show, of which John a Kent is accused, until he informs the lords that he has been busy

> . . . in an other place
> To tell ye trueth, against the Brydes should rise
> to sporte them with some pleasing vanities.
>
> ll. 888 ff.

Reminiscent of Friar Bacon and Friar Bungay, the two match wits in a demonstration which borrows from the progress entertainments. To disgrace John a Kent, John a Cumber arranges for a play to be presented by Turnop and his eager amateurs, and is assured of their "facilitie in your play or enterlude." Turnop, however, has qualms about the possible revenge of Kent, who does turn the tables by placing in the show the actual characters rather than actors impersonating them. John a Kent's agility is proved again in an ensuing morris dance, in which he eludes being made the fool, a role which falls upon John a Cumber. After crosses throughout the play, the two pairs of lovers are almost certainly united in marriage, although about thirty-five lines are probably lost from the final scene, where some fifty lines are imperfect.

Probably presented the following year, 1595, *A Midsummer Night's Dream* is compounded of similar ingredients: four crossed lovers, the love-chase, magic, and one subplot en-

tirely devoted to the preparation and presentation of a show
to celebrate a wedding. The undoubtedly popular rehearsal scene of Munday's play is extended fully by Shakespeare's
"hempen homespuns." Here are humorously represented all
the details of such amateur rehearsals which so harass a director: improvised properties, inadequate settings, the need
for additional dialogue, faulty readings, and the inevitable
self-styled genius who, like Turnop and Bottom, wants the
lion's share when the roles are assigned.[98] At the end of
A Midsummer Night's Dream, there is the hilarious presentation of the "enterlude," received with jests by the courtiers, but with indulgence by Theseus, who gently chides
the disparaging Philostrate:

> For never anything can be amiss
> When simpleness and duty tender it.
>
> V, i, 82 f.

And when Hippolyta complains, "He says they can do nothing
in this kind," Theseus, in the tradition of the ideal ruler mentioned above, replies:

> The kinder we, to give them thanks for nothing.
> Our sport shall be to take what they mistake;
> And what poor duty cannot do, noble respect
> Takes it in might, not merit.
>
> V, i, 88 ff.

In *Love's Labour's Lost,* which seems to be an earlier
play than *A Midsummer Night's Dream,* and may or not have
preceded *John a Kent,* the low comedy characters again are
integrated with the main plot by the device of an entertainment which they present. Here the situation closely approxi-
mates that of the progress, when the show was prepared by
the schoolmaster and performed by rustics before visiting
royalty. Armado comes directly to schoolmaster Holofernes to
announce:

. . . the King would have me present the Princess (sweet chuck) with some delightful ostentation, or show, or pageant, or antic, or firework. Now, understanding that the curate and your sweet self are good at such eruptions and sudden breaking-out of mirth, as it were, I have acquainted you withal, to the end to crave your assistance.

Immediately, Holofernes has the subject, a time-worn one:

Sir, you shall present before her the Nine Worthies.
V, i, 116 ff.

With considerable doubling, the show is to be enacted by the curate, Armado, Moth, Costard, and the schoolmaster himself. Just as the play of Pyramus and Thisbe may be a satire on the old-fashioned, bombastic dramas, so this display of the Nine Worthies in *Love's Labour's Lost* seems to ridicule one of the pageant's stock subjects. Such hardy perennials as the Virtues, the Nine Worthies, and the Labors of Hercules were as standard at the time of *Love's Labour's Lost* as they had been in 1578. At the latter date, directions were given in 2 *Promos and Cassandra* for the preparation of the following pageants to welcome the King:

> . . . up with the frame quickly,
> So space your roomes, as the nyne worthies may,
> Be so instauld, as best may please the eye.
> . . . .
>
> Let your man at Saynt Annes crosse, out of hande,
> Ereckt a stage, that the Wayghts in sight may stande.
> . . . .
>
> On Jesus gate, the foure vertues I trow,
> Appoynted are to stand:
>
> I, iv

The beadle reports that the Merchant Taylors' guild will present:

> . . . Hercules, of Monsters conqueryng
> Huge great Giants, in a forest fighting,

With Lyons, Beares, Wolues, Apes, Foxes and
    Grayes . . .

I, v

In the Nine Worthies Show in *Love's Labour's Lost,* the
style of the pageant verses is unmistakeably mirrored in Pompey's speech in septameter lines which are more intent upon
rime than reason:[99]

And travelling along this coast, I here am come
    by chance,
And lay my arms before the legs of this sweet lass of
    France.

V, ii, 557 f.

With the characteristic distraction of the amateur arranger,
Holofernes confuses the show of the labors of Hercules with
that of the Nine Worthies, and exhibits Hercules as one of
the historical worthies. By concession to the available talent,
this hero is presented at one of his infant labors. Strangling
the snake, the boy Moth stands mute, while the school-
master-presenter delivers an explanation embellished with the
classroom Latin so typical of the street shows:

Great Hercules is presented by this imp,
Whose club kill'd Cerberus, that three-headed canus;
And when he was a babe, a child, a shrimp,
Thus did he strangle serpents in his manus.

V, ii, 592 ff.

Far from Ben Jonson's ideal pageant where " 'Tis all in every
part," this show of the Nine Worthies parodies not only the
hackneyed subjects of the amateur shows, but the foolish
props, the poor speakers, the forced rime, limping metre
and needless explanation that "This is a Dog."

Following this Nine Worthies Show, Spring and Winter
enter to present a dialogue in praise of the Owl and the
Cuckoo, which Armado announces "should have followed

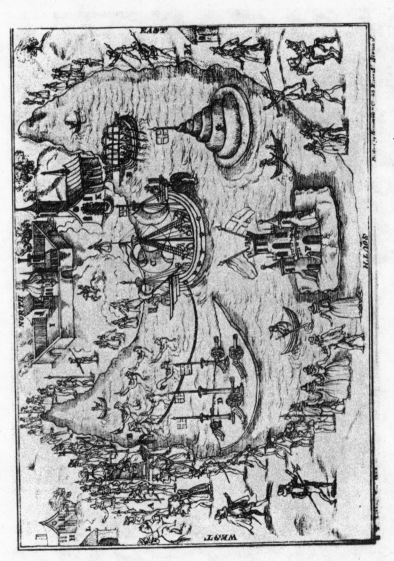

Plate VIII. Water pageantry, progress entertainment for Queen Elizabeth at Elvetham, 1591.

Plate IX. The "populous troops" of the royal progress train. A 16th-century tapestry depicting Catherine de Medici on progress.

in the end of our show."[100] By providing some of his best verse for this dialogue between Ver and Hiems, Shakespeare seems to imply that not all rural shows were awkward and comical. Some of them had real charm. Long popular in country entertainments, the debate between spring and winter had a ninth century prototype in the *Conflictus Veris et Hiemis*. According to Chambers, folk festivals celebrating by a mock battle the contest between spring and winter gave rise to the literary form of the *débat*, in which each side pleads its own advantages against the other,[101] as exemplified by the medieval work, "The Owl and the Nightingale." In the hands of the sophisticated courtiers, the simple *débat* developed into the elaborate *dubbio*, which was concerned with conflicting opinions regarding the more intriguingly immediate problems of love and etiquette, as reflected in *The Parliament of Fowles*, the "thirteen questions" in *Il Filocolo*, and *The Courtier*. Its popularity at court and adaptability of presentation led to the *dubbio's* becoming a feature of the progress entertainment. Thus, at Wanstead in 1578, the claims of a lady's suitor with "small deserts," i.e., little service to his lady, and no faults were weighed against those of his opponent who had many deserts and many faults. The *débat* was likewise a natural choice for the more ornate Tudor tilts, where action was instigated by literary argument. The opposing sides might be riches and love, as at an entertainment of the French ambassadors in 1528, or Desire and Virtue, as at a joust at Whitehall in 1581, also performed before an embassy from France.

In the drama, aspects of the *dubbi* can be seen in the works of John Lyly, who considers the rival claims of love, power and gold in *Midas*, of love and friendship in *Endymion* and *Euphues*, and of love and duty in *Alexander and Campaspe*. The relative merits of power, wisdom and love are argued by the three goddesses in Peele's *Arraignment of Paris.* A favorite debate of the courtiers was scholarship versus love, which was the subject of a joust celebrating the coronation of Henry VIII. Here, the scholars of Pallas contended with challengers who performed their feats for love. The same conflict between scholarship and love becomes a motif in *Love's Labour's Lost,* where the scholars' arguments at the opening of the play are rebutted by Berowne, whose eloquent defense of love is delivered at the end of the fourth act. Compared with such a debate, the simple beauty of the dialogue of Ver and Hiems may have seemed to sophisticates in the audience "harsh after the songs of Apollo."[102]

In depicting the audience at the amateur shows, the dramatists evidently held the mirror up to the nature of such courtiers as those at the "Bryde-ale" at Kenilworth. Laneham reported the royal train's hilarious reception of this unintentionally comic country show. In stage representation, the courtly spectators at an amateur offering increase the fun by firing witty remarks at the would-be actors, but the personage honored by the show is always kind. In *John A Kent,* Oswen warns Pembroke and others at the country reception,

> My Lordes, my father's tenants after their homely guise,
> welcome ye with their countrey merriment,
> How bad so ere, yet must ye needes accept it.

Pembroke replies,
> Else Oswen were we very much to blame . . .
>
> ll. 389 ff.

When the menials parade in, representing Fortune and her followers in *An Humorous Day's Mirth,* the stage audience gives full voice to its amusement. The start of the show itself is unfortunate: the Boy's speech of presentation is immediately interrupted by Labesha, questioning its facts. The complaisant Host wants to alter the speech; the Boy complains that he is "put out" and must begin all over again, to which the King responds, "With all my heart, 'tis so good we cannot heare it too oft."[103]

Likewise, the inept amateur shows are graciously received by Shakespeare's sovereigns, whose commendable behavior reflects Elizabeth's own. Theseus displays kind indulgence toward the tradesmen's "enterlude" in *A Midsummer Night's Dream,* and the conduct of the Princess at the Nine Worthies Show in *Love's Labour's Lost* is equally exemplary. While the others are unmercifully baiting the players (just as Theseus' courtiers berate Bottom and his crew), the Princess is encouraging and sympathetic:

> Great thanks, great Pompey.
>
> . . . .
>
> Alas, poor Maccabaeus, how hath he been baited!
> V, ii, 560; 634

In desperation, the vexed Armado appeals for attention to the Princess, who answers,

> Speak, brave Hector. We are much delighted.
> V, ii, 671

On the other hand, Dekker's *If It Be Not Good* exhibits the bad ruler who scorns the entertainment proferred by well-meaning subjects. Here, a good counselor wishes the King to view the shows which the people have prepared in his honor: The water bearers' May game; the Turners' show with a giant; and the presentations of the soldier, scholar and mariner. The last offering being especially recommended, the King agrees to witness it. However, his evil counselor, the devil in disguise, influences the ruler to abuse the devices. First the soldier comes in with his speech, is insulted by the King, and departs. It is then announced that a schoolmaster will present a "verie prettie show of his schollers in

broken Latin," but he leaves too, under the sovereign's ridicule. Likewise dismissed is the seaman, who

> Had rigd and mann'd 4. Gallies brauely furnisht
> With souldiers, Rowers, and fire-workes for a Sea-fight.

The good counselor departs, lamenting this unseemly treatment of the people by their ruler:

> Learning! and Armes! and Traffique! the triple wall
> That fortifies a Kingdome, race em downe Alle.

Members of the audience who might have been disappointed
when the anticipated shows failed to materialize, were re-
quited by a substitute show which the devil presented—fireworks from hell.[104]

Vortiger, in Middleton's *Mayor of Queenborough* similarly
exemplifies the bad sovereign. Among his other failings, he
is ungracious to subjects who wish to honor him by public
ceremony. "All the brethren," and the Mayor come to meet
the King and his train and to present a gift and a device, only
to be rudely shunned by Vortiger.

* * *

Since the Middle Ages, decorated city gates and landmarks
had been focal points of the splendor which attended public
occasions. In those early times, when the visual impression
served an important instructive function, a type of festive
public exhibition developed by which "living pictures" presented political, religious and moral themes. A main attraction
at public celebrations, these *tableaux vivants* grouped costumed and properted actors within an appropriate setting
upon an embellished landmark or city arch. This highly popular form which adorned sixteenth-century London on such

occasions as royal entries, Lord Mayors' Shows, and other civic festivities, suggested to Elizabethan dramatists details of subject matter and theme, as well as patterns of staging. Dumb shows, parades of personified abstractions, and tableaux reveal the technical influence of the pageants upon the plays. When the drama employed characteristic themes of the pageant, it frequently utilized as well, the established methods of presentation. Shakespeare perfectly blended these older elements into his plays to produce dramatically effective tableaux with political and moral implications, commented upon by an expositor.

The progress entertainments were pageants expanded in time and space. They were presented for the diversion of the Queen upon the country estates which she visited in the course of her summer progresses. A courtly audience would take delight in recognizing in a play such features of the progress entertainment as the arrival, welcome and shows in *The Arraignment of Paris* and the allegorical legend in Lyly's plays. Dramas designed for the private audience also reflected such characteristics of the entertainments as the water show and fireworks referred to by Oberon in *A Midsummer Night's Dream,* and the verses commemorating the hunt in *Love's Labour's Lost.* Amateur shows, like Falstaff's greeting of Henry V, were devised and presented by the citizens of London. However, these shows flourished in the country towns and on the estates, where the Queen's rustic subjects were invited to entertain her with a folk or morris dance, or mock joust, or even an "enterlude." The presence of such lowly figures is not incongruous then, in plays which reproduce conditions of the actual progress visits. Munday and Shakespeare integrate the courtly and comic levels by means of a subplot involving the preparation and presentation of an entertainment by "hempen homespuns."

CHAPTER FOUR

Shakespeare's Pageant Imagery

FIGURE AND FESTIVAL

WHEN THE HYMENEAL revels are over in *The Tempest,* and when the play itself, presented at a royal celebration, is drawing to a close, Prospero reflects upon "this insubstantial pageant faded."[1] Long ago, Malone felt that "the cloud-capp'd towers" "gorgeous places," "solemn temples," and "the great globe" suggested the triumphal arches which celebrated James' entry.[2] At that time, it will be recalled, Jonson's arch at Fenchurch was topped with a representation of London in little, with its houses, towers and steeples capped by clouds which dispersed at the approach of the King. Another arch by Jonson rose in the form of the Temple of Janus, while a huge globe of the world revolved in a pageant in Fleet Street. Other scholars have found the passage provocatively reminiscent of royal display. Enid Welsford believes that Prospero is thinking of theatrical staging and street pageantry,[3] and Allardyce Nicoll proposes the masque as the source for this imagery.[4] Since all agree that the passage's employment of spectacle contributes to its philosophical implications as well as to its aesthetic appeal, it should prove rewarding to examine more closely Shakespeare's use of the street pageant as a source of imagery here and elsewhere. Not only the pageant, but the entry, the welcome and the progress entertainment, provided an abundant field of reference for imagery to delight the mind's eye of the spectator just as his actual vision was served by the stage spectacle. In antithesis to Homer, who employed pictures of simple daily life to make the splendor of palaces and armies comprehensible to his audience, Shakespeare stirred his listeners by allusions to festive display, which not only clarified but colored his lines by reflecting the decoration and allegory of the pageant and progress entertainment.

The *tableaux vivants* provided special effects in imagery as well as in staging. When Richard III piously posed between two bishops, or Henry V stood clasping the hand of the Justice, the audience witnessed a familiar pageant: the tableau of personified virtues surrounding a pageant sovereign. In descriptive verse, that literary storehouse of pageantry and tableaux, *The Faerie Queene,* presents a similiar effect at the trial of Duessa, where the maiden Queen, Mercilla, representing Elizabeth, is seated with virgins around her, Temperance and Reverence as her attendants, and a lion under her feet.[5] Fortune and Envy were the popular villains in the pageants depicting the sovereign protected by virtues and immune from dangers. At James' entry, for instance, the King's Virtue was mounted above Fortune and beyond the reach of Envy. These same pageant figures assume their customary tableau in an image in *Titus Andronicus,* when Aaron the Moor envisions the position of the newly-crowned Empress Tamora:

> Now climbeth Tamora Olympus' top,
> Safe out of Fortune's shot, and sits aloft,

> Secure of thunder's crack or lightning flash,
> Advanc'd above pale envy's threat'ning reach.
>
> II, i, 1 ff.

In addition to personified abstractions, mythological deities and historical worthies took their places in the pageant along with the representations of the sovereign honored. Thus an entering monarch might see himself flatteringly portrayed as the nonpareil ruler, or as a personified virtue, or as a hero of history or legend. On occasion, a pageant provided a place for the honored personage, but his participation in the show, as opposed to his partaking in the private masque, was rare. A device presented to Prince Arthur and Catherine of Aragon in 1501 at the entrance of St. Paul's exhibited the Virtues, above whom Honor sat enthroned, with an empty seat at either side, designated for the Prince and his bride. Prince Francis, the Duke of Anjou, actually mounted the pageant stage, according to an English pamphlet describing his reception at Antwerp in 1581. After alighting from his horse and ascending a forty-foot scaffold, the Prince took his place in an elaborately decorated chair, flanked by pillars and symbolical animals. But only she of "infinite variety" is both the entrant and the pageant, as into view glides the decorated barge of Cleopatra *en tableau* as Venus, with Cupids, Nereides, and Graces grouped about her:

> The barge she sat in like a burnish'd throne,
> Burn'd on the water. The poop was beaten gold;
> Purple the sails, and so perfumed that
> The winds were lovesick with them; the oars were silver,
> Which to the tune of flutes kept stroke, and made
> The water which they beat to follow faster,
> As amorous of their strokes. For her own person,
> It beggar'd all description. She did lie
> In her pavilion, cloth-of-gold of tissue,

O'erpicturing that Venus where we see
The fancy outwork nature. On each side her
Stood pretty dimpled boys, like smiling Cupids,
With divers-colour'd fans, whose wind did seem
To glow the delicate cheeks which they did cool,
And what they undid did . . . .
Her gentlewomen, like the Nereides,
So many mermaids, tended her i' th' eyes,
And made their bends adornings. At the helm
A seeming mermaid steers.

II, ii, 196 ff.

Surely Shakespeare's audience was reminded not so much of Roman history as of English pageantry along the Thames. According to North's translation of Plutarch's *Lives,* before Antony went to Cilicia, he sent to command Cleopatra to appear personally before him there, to answer charges that she had aided Cassius and Brutus in their war against him. The messenger, " when he had considered her beauty," advised her to come into Cilicia "as honorably furnished as she could possible." North continues,

When she was sent unto . . . . she made so light and mocked *Antonius* so much that she disdained to set forward otherwise, but to take her barge in the riuer of Cydnus, the poope whereof was of gold, the sailes of purple, and the owers of siluer, which kept stroke in rowing after the sound of the musicke . . . . And now for the person of her selfe: she was laide vnder a pauillion of cloth of golde of tissue, apparelled and attired like the goddesse *Venus* . . . on either hand of her, pretie faire boyes apparelled as painters doe set foorth god *Cupide.* . . . Her Ladies and gentlewomen also . . . were apparelled like the nymphes *Nereides* (which are the myrmaides of the waters) and like the Graces . . .[6]

It is not difficult to imagine Cleopatra slyly deciding to present Antony with a welcoming show for which the crowd would—as it did—desert the conqueror to throng to gaze at the pageant on the water. And since symbolism was customary in pageantry, what better subject than Venus for Cleopatra to present to the "plated Mars" who "Enthron'd i' th' market place, did sit alone"? It will be noted that while Shakespeare changes little of North's picture, he does omit the graces attendant on Cleopatra, perhaps because they are more indigenous to land pageants, such as the welcome at Elvetham and the New Arabia at James' entry. North too makes clear that Cleopatra not only resembled Venus, but was "attired like the goddesse Venus."

Cleopatra is fond of staging herself to the public's eyes. Later in the play, in a passage again based upon North, Caesar describes how Antony and Cleopatra have displayed themselves in Egypt:

> I' th' market place on a tribunal silver'd
> Cleopatra and himself in chairs of gold
> Were publicly enthron'd.

Their children were arranged at their feet. And Cleopatra

> In th' habiliments of the goddess Isis
> That day appear'd;
>
> III, vi, 3 ff.

No sooner has Octavius painted for the audience this sumptuous picture of Cleopatra than his sparsely-attended sister, Antony's wife, enters, to be chided for coming so unostentatiously, like "a market-maid to Rome."[7]

As in her first appearance before Antony, Cleopatra at the end of the play dies *en tableau*. She gives orders for her "best attires," announces, "I am again for Cydnus,"[8] and expires in carefully-arranged glory, royally robed, crowned, and enthroned, with Iris dead at her feet and Charmian standing behind her.

While the description of Cleopatra in her barge fully pictures a specific water pageant, frequently the general appearance of a splendid fleet might be described in terms of the sea shows. For example, in the following passage from *The Merchant of Venice,* Salarnio remarks that Antonio's "argosies with portly sail,"[9]

Like signiors and rich burghers on the flood,
Or, as it were, the pageants of the sea—
Do overpeer the petty traffickers,
That cursy to them, do them reverence,
As they fly by them with their woven wings.

I, i, 10 ff.

It has been suggested that the passage alludes to the pageant devices of huge ships which were drawn about in street shows and thus dwarfed the spectators, the "petty traffickers."[10] Exemplifying the Gargantuan dimensions which these devices sometimes attained, were the pageant whale, twenty-seven feet in length by fifteen feet in height and the similarly oversized ship, the measurements of which were recorded in the report of an Antwerp festival.[11] However, Shakespeare may have confined the image to the water and the actual "pageants of the sea." Thus, the passage would draw an imaginative comparison between the colorfully decorative pageant barges floating past the plain and reverential traffickers, and Antonio's argosy, which likewise outshines the ordinary ships upon the sea. Frequently sponsored by the "rich burghers" of the guilds, water pageantry would be an especially appropriate allusion in a play concerning a merchant.

The association of a fleet of ships with a pageant is not uncommon. The Armada is described as ". . .Warlike Pageants dancing on the waves," in Dekker's *The Whore of Babylon.*[12] In *Othello,* there is reference to both the splendor and the appeal of the water shows when the heading of Turkish galleys towards Rhodes rather than Cyprus is regarded by the First Senator as a pageant "To keep us in false gaze."[13] Sometimes,

a fleet of ships might suggest a city upon the waves, an image
Shakespeare employs in *Henry V*:

> Suppose that you have seen
> The well-appointed King at Hampton pier
> Embark his royalty; and his brave fleet
> With silken streamers the young Phoebus fanning.
> . . . .
> O, do but think
> You stand upon the rivage and behold
> A city on th' inconstant billows dancing;
> For so appears this fleet majestical . . .
>
> III, Ch., 3 ff.

In the case of actual sea pageantry, the effect of a floating
city was pronounced when the barges, like the one James presented to King Christian, were formed to resemble castles,
fortresses, and other buildings.

The water shows at the progress entertainments might provide a source for imagery, as in the passage cited earlier, from
A Midsummer Night's Dream, where Oberon paints a highly imaginative picture of the origin of the flower of love.
Those who were acquainted with the estate entertainments
no doubt took special delight in recognizing in the speech
such features as the mermaid on a dolphin's back, the fireworks, and the royal, chaste vestal, seated by the west.

Sometimes it was not the pageant as an entity, but one of
its particular aspects, from which an image would be drawn.
Thus, while many of the allusions in the Elizabethan drama
have become exclusively literary today, they suggested to the
original audience specific visual images. The numerous references to giants, for instance, required no especial feats of
the imagination on the part of the listener who had seen such
massive pageant figures towed through the streets at civic celebrations. Likewise, these spectators had encountered in the
street shows most of the personified abstractions who might

appear or be alluded to in the drama. The men and women of Shakespeare's audience had seen a leafy, flourishing bower exhibited to depict a prospering commonwealth, and they had seen a decaying garden displayed to represent a badly governed country. The mention of a conduit or city gate in connection with a king would almost invariably carry an association with the pageants which were mounted upon these landmarks to celebrate the ruler. Some of this original vividness of impression may be recaptured by considering Shakespeare's images and allusions in their relationship to the pageant.

Symbolic of the parade itself were the two figures who marched at its head: the whiffler who cleared the way for the procession, and the marshal who led it. Thus, in *Henry V*, when the King's decorated fleet sails in triumph to England from the victory at Agincourt, the "deep-mouth'd sea" parts before the royal ship and

> . . . like a mighty whiffler fore the King,
> Seems to prepare his way.
>
> V, Ch., 11 ff.

More subtly effective is the association of the marshal's sword or staff with Macbeth's motives just before he kills Duncan. "Thou marshall'st me the way that I was going,"[14] he utters to the dagger by which he is to gain the pomp of sovereignty with which we see him invested in the following act. The hallucination symbolizes not only the desirable end, however, but the violent means, for it first suggests the sword of the marshal who led the stately parades of kingship, and then, covered with blood it reminds Macbeth of the terrifying manner by which he is to arrive at the path of glory. With characteristic vividness of imagination, Macbeth has fixed upon a symbol representative of the conflict within him between ambition for worldly pomp, and horror at the inhuman deed necessary for its attainment.

While the whiffler and the marshal were more or less representative of the procession as a whole, many individual characters and features of the pageants colored Shakespeare's imagery. In the history of the pageant, perhaps the most popular single figure was the giant, beloved member of the earliest folk festivals and civic celebrations in England and on the continent. In England, the guilds in the provinces had their own giants, such as the one displayed by the Coventry Cappers' Company.[15] One London citizen's delight in the pageant giants is reflected in the diary of Henry Machyn, which carefully recorded appearances of these popular figures at city festivities. In 1553 he noted, for instance, that there "cam through. . .gyants boyth great and smalle," while in 1559, "sant John Sacerys, with a gyant," the Nine Worthies and "a goodly pagant," were displayed.[16]

In his legendary background, the giant reflected the interest of the Elizabethans in the honorable antiquity of their race. According to the legend, their Trojan ancestor, Brute, arrived at the island of England to find it ruled by the giant Albion, whom the hero fought and slew. Then, according to one version, Albion's giant brothers, Gog and Magog, (later one giant, Gogmagog) were taken prisoner and led in triumph through London. After this, they were chained as porters at the gate of the palace built on the spot where Guildhall later was constructed, displaying at its entrance stone figures of Gogmagog and Brutus' brother Corineus (who in some versions was the slayer of Albion.)[17] Thus, the pageant giants were customarily attired in Roman dress, whether they represented Trojan conquerors or members of classical mythology or local legend. At Elizabeth's coronation festivities, Temple Bar displayed two huge giants, representing Gogmagog the Albion and Corineus the Briton, who was, of course, equally gigantic. In *Locrine,* which concerns the early history of Britain, Corineus recounts his fight with Gogmagog, whose gigantic figure had impressed members of the audience in pageants and statuary.

The giant figure was almost always a feature of the midsummer shows, whose pageantry was later taken over by the annual festivities celebrating the newly-elected Lord Mayor.[18] Puttenham contributes some incidental information regarding the construction of the midsummer giants. In drawing a rhetorical comparison, he mentions "these midsomer pageants in London, where to make the people wonder are set forth great and vglie Gyants marching as if they were aliue, and armed at all points, but within they are stuffed full of browne paper and tow. . . ."[19] That the giant retained its popularity in the Lord Mayors' Shows is reflected in *The Dutch Courtesan,* where it is suggested to Crispinella that she wear shoes elevated with soles of cork to increase her height. She replies that she does walk in chopines "and yet all will scarce make me so high as one of the Gyants stilts that stalkes before my Lord Maiors pageant."[20]

Giant figures sometimes towered over the estates at progress time. Representing the huge early inhabitants of England were the eight-foot trumpeters at Kenilworth, where "by this dum shew it was ment, that in the daies and reigne of King Arthure, men were of that stature; so that the Castle of Kenelworth should seeme still to be kept by Arthur's heires . . . " [21]

In the drama, an allusion to giants would recall concretely the Gargantuan figures, attired in Roman dress, who stalked through the London streets in the Lord Mayors' Shows or other festivities. No doubt contributing to the impression of Bussy D'Ambois as a dominant figure in Chapman's play are the many references to giants in connection with the hero. Bussy is likened to Atlas and to the Giant Typhon, and in his first appearance, the hero reflects on the resemblance between men who are "meerely great" and the Colossus. At the end of the play, Bussy recalls the huge figures in statuary, by affirming that he will stand "like a Roman statue . . . 'till death hath made me marble."[22] The same comparison had been made previously in *Tamburlaine,* with a similarly impressive effect. Here, the hero is actually described as a giant-like figure, when Menaphon depicts Tamburlaine as a Hercules who "might mainely bear Old Atlas burthen," and whose eyes in their

> . . . fiery cyrcles beare encompassed
> A heauen of heauenly bodies in their Spheares:
> That guides his steps and actions to the throne,
> Where honor sits inuested royally:
> Pt. 1, II, i, 464 ff.

In the same vein, Cleopatra describes the Antony of her dreams as a gigantic figure:

> His face was as the heav'ns, and therein stuck
> A sun and moon, which kept their course and lighted
> The little O, the earth . . . .
> His legs bestrid the ocean: his rear'd arm
> Crested the world. His voice was propertied
> As all the tuned spheres, and that to friends;
> But when he meant to quail and shake the orb,
> He was as rattling thunder. For his bounty,
> There was no winter in't; an autumn 'twas
> That grew the more by reaping. His delights
> Were dolphin-like: they show'd his back above
> The element they liv'd in. In his livery
> Walk'd crowns and crownets. Realms and islands were
> As plates dropp'd from his pocket.
> V, ii, 79 ff.

As far back as 1794, features of the pageant in this passage were pointed out by Walter Whiter, who stated,

Let it be remembered that an imitation of the sphere of the Heavens, with the attributes and ornaments belonging to it, the sweetness of its music and the noise of its thunder, the Sun, the Moon, and the Earth, colossal figures—armorial bearings—a magnificent procession of monarchs and their attendants—floating islands—and a prodigal distribution of wealth and honors, are the known and familiar materials, which formed the motley compound of the Masque, the Pageant or the Procession.[23]

Cleopatra's final tribute skillfully employs elements of the pageant to recall Antony's greatness and magnificence, which throughout the play have counterpoised his slavery to passion.

Not all of the giants were attired as Romans. Some, drawn perhaps from legend and myth, were more fanciful. An Eastern giant figure is suggested in an image in *Cymbeline*:

> The gates of monarchs
> Are arch'd so high that giants may jet through
> And keep their impious turbands on without
> Good morrow to the sun.
>
> III, iii, 4 ff.

In Antwerp, one actual pageant giant was less lucky, for his exceptional height prevented him from getting through the city gates to be displayed in parades in other communities.[24]

Like the giants, the personified abstractions alluded to or represented by the dramatists required no wild flights of the imagination on the part of the members of the audience. These men and women needed no acquaintance with Ben Jonson's handbook, the *Iconologia* of Cesar Ripa, which prescribed the characteristic properties, costume, position and companions for a standard personification.[25] Illustrated in the popular emblem books and referred to in literature, these figures had made their stage debuts in the pageants, before the same class of spectators who later applauded them in drama and dumb show—the citizens. At the beginning of *Old Fortunatus*, the throned lady with her wheel and the globe at her feet would be recognized immediately as Fortune, while a character entering in a robe "painted full of tongues" at the opening of 2 *Henry IV* would be promptly identified as Rumor by many in the audience. By the same type of association, allusions to personified abstractions would be likely to call up concrete images in the minds of hearers who had formerly seen these figures exhibited on the pageant stage.

Perhaps it was through the influence of the street shows that the political personified abstractions succeeded the ethical in popularity. In the Middle Ages, Englishmen had been accustomed to seeing such characters in the morality plays as the Vice, the Seven Deadly Sins, and the Cardinal Virtues. Concerned with King and Commonwealth rather than with Everyman, the Renaissance pageant employed personifications depicting the various countries, Peace, Plenty, Rumor, Dissension, Detraction, Zeal, etc.

The figures of Peace and Plenty were as frequently alluded to in the political dramas as they were displayed in the pageants concerning similar subjects. In *The Whore of Babylon*, Dekker depicts England as an ideal country, where "Peace (here) eats fruits, which her own hand hath sown," and the land is husbanded by Providence, Zeal and Integritie.[26] At the end of *Richard III*, Richmond likewise calls on "smooth-fac'd peace" and "smiling plenty"[27] to attend upon his future heirs. And Cranmer in *Henry VIII* prophesies of Elizabeth that, "Truth shall nurse her," and at her death,

Peace, plenty, love, truth, terror,

That were the servants to this chosen infant,
Shall then be his . . . [James']

V, v, 48 ff.

While the age of allegory personified abstract qualities, it
endowed the commonplace and familiar with a symbolical
significance. In this attempt to present the abstract and mys-
tic in concrete, comprehensible form, the visual arts, including the pageant, played a major role. Not only did the street
shows present allegorical figures, but they also depicted the
animal and nature symbolism of the Middle Ages. In early
religious pageants, symbolic animals were displayed, the
phoenix representing the resurrection, and the pelican representing the passion, not to mention the apostolic ox, eagle
and lion. Probably such exhibitions influenced the use of
animals with a heraldic significance in the pageants of genealogy mentioned above, and in the later Lord Mayors' Shows,
where a chariot with allegorical figures mounted upon it
might be drawn by the heraldic fauna of the guild. In their
1616 show, the Fishmongers, who had dolphins and luces on
their coats of arms, displayed a crowned dolphin with Arion
on its back. The Goldsmiths, whose crest bore a leopard and
unicorns, were honored in the same show by a display of the
Emperor of Morocco upon a golden leopard.[28] Nicholas Breton
mentions a parade of such pageant animals in *Cornu-copiae*:

When as the Pageants through Chepe-side are carried,
. . . .
If then you marke when as the fire-workes flye,
And Elephants and Vnicornes passe by,
How mighty and tumultuous is that presse . . .[29]

According to a medieval hierarchy, the highest degree
among the animals was held by the lion, among birds by the
eagle, in the planets, by the sun, and among men by the king.
This would account for the numerous literary allusions to

the king as the sun, an eagle or a lion. Just as this same symbolism was visually portrayed by the pageants honoring the
sovereign, so was it employed in dramatic passages concerned
with a royal show or display. In *Richard II,* for instance,
Bolingbroke arrives at Flint Castle to confront Richard, who
appears upon the walls *en tableau* with the Bishop of Carl-
isle, Aumerle, Scroop, and Salisbury. Bolingbroke remarks,

> See, see, King Richard doth himself appear,
> As doth the blushing discontented sun
> From out the fiery portal of the East
> When he perceives the envious clouds are bent
> To dim his glory and to stain the track
> Of his bright passage to the Occident.

To which York replies:

> Yet looks he like a king. Behold, his eye,
> As bright as is the eagle's, lightens forth
> Controlling majesty. Alack, alack, for woe,
> That any harm should stain so fair a show!
>
> III, iii, 62 ff.

The use of the sun as a symbol of the king was turned to
striking visual effect in pageantry, where the writers employed
such ingenious devices as gardens flourishing at the sun-king's
approach, or clouds lifting from a mock-city when he appeared. Throughout *Richard III,* images of the sun and the
clouds reflect the fortunes of the House of York. In the opening passage of the play, Richard employs a favorite device
of the royal entry pageant when he rejoices that the recently-
crowned sun-king has dispersed

> . . . all the clouds that low'rd upon our house.
>
> I, i, 3

Near the end of the play, Richard muses,

> The sun will not be seen to-day;
> The sky doth frown and low'r upon our army.
>
> V, iii, 282 f.

It was only fitting that Shakespeare should liken the splendor of the sun to that of the king on his public appearances. Thus, in 1 *Henry IV*, the ruler advises his son to appear "seldom but sumptuous" in the eye of a public sated by the sight of the skipping King Richard, which did

> Afford no extraordinary gaze,
> Such as is bent on sunlike majesty
> When it shines seldom in admiring eyes;
>
> III, ii, 78 ff.

Perhaps the King recalls his father's instructions when he warns the Dauphin in *Henry V*:

> . . . I will keep my state,
> Be like a king, and show my sail of greatness,
> When I do rouse me in my throne of France.
>
> .   .   .   .
>
> . . . I will rise there with so full a glory
> That I will dazzle all the eyes of France.
>
> I, ii, 273 ff.

In addition to the metaphorical association of the sun and the public-appearing king, any reference to the royal entry would invariably suggest the city gates or arches decorated in celebration of the sumptuous occasion. Interesting images result from Shakespeare's association of the sun-king and the city gate. Thus, in the above-mentioned image from *Cymbeline*, he refers to the gates of monarchs through which impious giants pass "without good morrow to the sun." A more extensive and complex association of the sun and the gate colors a passage in *Troilus and Cressida*:

> . . . no man is the lord of anything,
> Though in and of him there be much consisting,
> Till he communicate his parts to others;
> Nor doth he of himself know them for aught
> Till he behold them formed in th' applause
> Where th' are extended, who, like an arch, reverb'rate

The voice again; or, like a gate of steel
Fronting the sun, receives and renders back
His figure and his heat.

III, iii, 115 ff.

To the Elizabethan hearers, the literal meaning of this passage was enriched by its overtones of the royal entry: the public appreciation and applause of virtue, the reverberation of
the voice when one passes beneath the archway, the sun as a
synonym for the king whose figure (usually surrounded by
virtues) is reproduced in a show on the arch, and which
figure is thus, like an actual reflection "rendered back" to
the sovereign observing and honored by the pageant.

Many of Shakespeare's images, as Caroline Spurgeon has
noted, treat the royal family in terms of the tree or plant.[30]
As mentioned, the genealogical tree was almost a fixture of
the coronation pageant displaying the new king's rightful
title to the throne. While the pageant symbolized the family
by trees or plants, it often employed a flourishing or fading
bower to represent the state of the commonwealth, as displayed with great elaboration by the Garden of Plenty arch
at James' entry (See Plate III). Sometimes, in place of a bower
to represent the state, show makers used two trees or plants,
one blooming, the other drooping. At Elizabeth's entry, for
instance, a pageant depicted a decaying and a thriving commonwealth by means of a stony hill with a withered tree, and
a fair flowered mound with a green tree.[31] As reported by an
English pamphlet, the festivities with which the Duke of Anjou was received at Antwerp utilized a similar theme. In one
pageant, Apollo and the nine muses inhabited the flourishing bower of Mount Parnassus, while across the street, in a
pageant of dry and withered trees, lurked the hellhounds of
Discord, Violence, and Tyranny. Some effective dramatic
imagery is founded upon the same comparison of the com-

monwealth to a bower. In *The True Tragedy of Richard III,*
the government of the state is alluded to as a "sauage, shultred
groue,"[32] while in *The Whore of Babylon* it is feared that
foreign influence will cause England's fairy bowers to turn
to Arabian deserts.[33] This metaphor of the state as a garden
could be extended to include the image of the beneficial sun
as the sovereign. Enemies of the bower-country were depicted
appropriately. Bolingbroke in *Richard II* refers to Bushy,
Bagot and their accomplices as

> The caterpillars of the commonwealth,
> Which I have sworn to weed and pluck away.
>> II, iii, 166 f.

The prospering commonwealth also was represented in
pageants as a flourishing island or "paradise," filled with
fruits and flowers, an ideal presentation for the grocers'
guild. A famous passage in *Richard II* employs the figure
of the flourishing isle, praised as "this other Eden, demi-para-
dise," and a "precious stone set in the silver sea."[34] Later, in
the garden scene, there is an extended analogy of the commonwealth to an island bower which has fallen into ruin:

> . . . our sea-walled garden, the whole land,
> Is full of weeds, her fairest flowers chok'd up,
> Her fruit trees all unprun'd, her hedges ruin'd,
> Her knots disordered, and her wholesome herbs
> Swarming with caterpillars.
>> III, iv, 43 ff.

A popular method of indicating the prosperity of the nation
was to fill the conduits with wine, a practice common at
many public celebrations of royalty. Like the arches, the conduits which bore pageants and ran with wine at the royal entries were associated with the ruler in imagery and allusion.
In *The Winter's Tale,* the gentleman recounting the final re-
conciliation describes "the old shepherd, which stands by like

a weather-bitten conduit of many kings' reigns."[35] An exceedingly grim image of a conduit running red wine may be suggested in *Titus Andronicus*, when the bleeding Lavinia with her tongue cut out and her hands cut off, is described by Marcus as "a conduit with three issuing spouts."[36] When Jack Cade claims the throne in 2 *Henry VI*, he announces that the conduit is to run with wine for an entire year.[37]

Wine in the conduits is only one of the customs of the royal entry which are decreed by Cade—there must be a procession into London, "where we will have the mayor's sword borne before us;" he will enter in triumph as did the Roman heroes, and the bodies of his enemies "shall be dragg'd at my horse heels till I do come to London."[38] Cade's appropriating the usually ceremonious formal entry accentuates the threat of terror to the city of London under the rule of the rabble. Here Shakespeare is using details of the splendid entry for contrast with a somber situation, as he does also in *Richard III*. In *Hamlet* and *Coriolanus*, this same contrast is subtly employed in imagery based upon the entry.

His lament that "the world is out of joint," strikes a note recurrent in many of Hamlet's own images. These concern an object or idea usually associated with joy or beauty, but now viewed in the distorted and ugly focus into which Hamlet's world has been cast by the affairs of his life. Such images are based upon the paradox of an unnatural transformation of the normal good or beauty characteristic of a particular object or quality, for instance:

solid flesh. . .melt, Thaw, and resolve itself into a dew!

goodly frame, the earth. . .a sterile promontory;

. . .native hue of resolution. . .sicklied o'er with the pale cast of thought,

. . .transform honesty from what it is to a bawd. . .

Virtue itself of vice must pardon beg—

. . .godlike reason To fust in us unus'd.[39]

Having been deprived of the throne by his uncle's election, Hamlet phrases some of his thoughts in terms of the royal entry and progresses which might have been his, but he twists the features of the usually joyous occasions. Suspicious of the plot against his life, Hamlet employs the whifflers and marshal of his usurped royal entry to describe his own dark and lonely journey *from* the kingdom:

> There's letters seal'd; and my two schoolfellows,
> Whom I will trust as I will adders fang'd,
> They bear the mandate; they must sweep my way
> And marshal me to knavery.
>
> III, iv, 202 ff.

The whiffler's duty of clearing a path for the procession is associated with the sweeping movements of deadly snakes, to which he compares Rosencrantz and Guildenstern; these deceitful creatures will lead him not, like the marshal, to a throne, but to unknown evil, perhaps death. A similar contrast combines the gilded royal ceremony with the grimmest of realism in Hamlet's startling reminder to his uncle, "how a king may go a progress through the guts of a beggar."[40]

Likewise, in *Coriolanus*, the royal entry suggests an image founded upon contrast. This contrast is neither imaginative nor associative as in *Hamlet*, but actual, for the victor who brings triumph and joy to his own city has of necessity brought death and destruction to another. Thus, as the trumpets sound, just before the spectacular entry of Marcius, Volumnia remarks that "Before him he carries noise, and behind him he leaves tears."[41] In the next scene, Cominius describes Coriolanus' storming of the gates of Corioli, for which the triumph was held in Rome:

> From face to foot
> He was a thing of blood, whose every motion
> Was tim'd with dying cries. Alone he ent'red
> The mortal gate of th' city, which he painted
> With shunless destiny;
>
> II, ii, 112 ff.

Here Shakespeare employs the details of a triumphal entry to describe an entry in conquest. The splendor and joy of the former is replaced by the grief and misery of the latter. Like an entering hero, Coriolanus is especially attired—but in blood. Instead of the music which accompanied the triumph, his "every motion was tim'd with dying cries."[42] For the citizens of Corioli, the gate through which the conqueror entered might be as "mortal" (or deadly) as the gate of the underworld. These gates are not only "mortal"; they are also "painted," like those which decorated the royal entries. Here, in place of the customarily optimistic scene, Coriolanus displays upon the gate "shunless destiny," the triumph of fate. In sharp contrast to the usual throngs at an entry, his solitary figure foreshadows Coriolanus' later departure alone from his own city which he has just entered in triumph when this description is delivered.

Just as his staged entries and exits represent the veering fortunes of Coriolanus, so is the imagery balanced for effect. In Act IV, another conquest is described in terms of the entry, but this time the implications are even graver, for it is his own city which Coriolanus seeks to destroy. Speaking of Coriolanus' forthcoming attack upon Rome, one of the servants employs such features of the entry as the porter at the gate and the whiffler who clears the way:

He'll go, he says, and sole [i.e., pull] the porter of Rome gates by th' ears. He will mow all down before him and leave his passage poll'd [cleared].

> IV, v, 213 ff.

In keeping with the pattern of contrasts in *Coriolanus,* where
the staged triumph in Rome is followed by the departure in
disgrace, and the conquests of Corioli and Rome are depicted
in terms of the joyful entry, Coriolanus' second entry into
Corioli balances his former one as related by Cominius. He
appears "marching with Drum and Colours, the Commoners
being with him," to proclaim peace, but is declared a traitor.
Reminded of his last entry to their city, the people desert the
hero and join the conspirators in calling for Coriolanus'
death.[43] The play ends with his funeral march.

PETRACH'S *TRIONFI*

WHEN ROGER ASCHAM complains that "Englishmen Italian-
ated" "have in more Reverence the Triumphs of Petrarch
than the Genesis of Moses,"[44] the *Triumphs* is not an
idle choice for his example. In England, where a translation
appeared in 1554, and upon the continent, Petrarch's *Trionfi*
greatly influenced art and literature, and pervaded the fields
of festival and drama. This widespread popularity was due in
part to the exploitation of the *Triumphs* by the visual arts.
At first, woodcuts and engravings appeared, illustrating the
text by portraying the successive triumphs of Love, Chastity,
Death, Fame, Time and Eternity, and soon such artists as
Bonifazio Veneziano and Lorenzo Costa were employing the
theme in their paintings.[45] Tapestry makers took up the subject; the walls at Wolsey's Hampton Court displayed colorful and elaborate tapestries of all six triumphs.[46] Later, when
Prince Charles went to Spain, he found the Queen's quarter
"all hung with Tapistrie of Tunys, and Petrarckes triumphs

set forth in embroyderie . . ."[47] On the popular level, these triumphs provided a recurrent motif for decoration, and were represented upon marriage chests, dishes, miniatures, and even monuments.

The influence worked both ways. While Petrarch employed as a frame for his work the public "triumphs" or festivals of his time, his poem introduced a new allegorical theme for future celebrations. The combination of the classical and allegorical triumphs was demonstrated in actual practice at the entry of Alfonso the Great to Naples in 1443 in the style of a Roman Emperator. The procession followed the classical models, but its participants, like those in Petrarch's poem, included allegorical, historical, and mythological characters. Taking part in the parade were the figures of Fortune in a chariot, and the Seven Virtues on horseback. Crowned with laurel and mounted above a revolving globe, an actor representing Julius Caesar explained the symbolic devices to Alfonso.[48] The allegorical triumph introduced a new figure into eulogies welcoming the ruler. When Elizabeth arrived at Bisham in 1592, a shepherdess hailed her coming:

This way commeth the Queene. . .Nature's glory, leading affections in fetters, Virginitie's slaves: embracing mildnes with justice, Majestie's twinns. . . .One hande she stretcheth to Fraunce, to weaken Rebels; the other to Flaunders, to strengthen Religion. . . .this is shee at whom Envie hath shot all her arrowes, and now for anger broke her bow. . . .Heedlesse Treason goeth hedlesse; and close Trechery restlesse: Daunger looketh pale to behold her Majestie; and Tyranny blusheth to heare of her mercy.[49]

Thus, the word "triumph" in the Renaissance applied not only to magnificent and splendid parades of a warrior in Roman fashion, in a chariot, crowned with laurel, followed by prisoners and the army, with trophies and exotic animals included in the entourage. Similar processions with alle-

gorical features were likewise termed "triumphs," and finally,
in England, the word came to be used as a synonym for
"pageant," and more loosely, to signify a splendid celebration
which might or might not include allegorical representations.
Thus York asks his son in *Richard II*, "What news from Oxford? Do these justs and triumphs hold?"[50]

The triumph form which Petrarch chose had been employed in literature as well as in life.[51] The most prominent
literary example in his own day was the Triumph of Revelation with which Dante introduced Beatrice in "Purgatorio."
At the head of this allegorical religious procession come
twenty-four singing elders, representing the twenty-four books
of the Old Testament, and the apostolic animals surround the
triumphal chariot of the church in which Beatrice, Divine
Revelation, is drawn by a griffin. Three ladies, Charity, Hope
and Faith, dance a measure at the right wheel and at the left
the four Cardinal Virtues "make festival." Following the
chariot come Luke and Paul, then James, Peter, John and
Jude, and finally, a solitary, keen-visioned old man "in a
trance," John, the author of Revelations.[52]

Among the classical writers, Plato employs a procession of
gods in the "Phaedrus." In attempting to explain the nature
of the soul, Socrates describes a festal parade in heaven,
headed by the winged chariot of Zeus, who is followed by
a host of gods and inferior deities in eleven divisions.[53] Likewise Lucretius in *De Rerum Natura* depicts a pagan allegorical religious procession celebrating the earth goddess:

> Seated in chariot o'er the realms of air
> To drive her team of lions. . .
> .   .   .   .
> .   .   .   .   .Unto her car
> They've yoked the wild beasts, since a progeny,
> However savage, must be tamed and chid

By care of parents. They have girt about
With turret-crown the summit of her head,
Since, fortressed in her goodly strongholds high,
'Tis she sustains the cities; now, adorned
With that same token, to-day is carried forth,
With solemn awe through many a mighty land,
The image of that mother, the divine.[54]

Like his *Canzoniere* and Dante's *Vita Nuova* and *Commedia*, Petrarch's *Trionfi* celebrates the final triumph of spiritual love, or the love of God, over physical love, or the love of mortals. In the poem, Petrarch first encounters the Triumph of Love, in which Cupid's chariot is followed by a procession of his bound captives. As in the pageants, figures from the Bible, classical mythology, legend, history and allegory mingle freely in the *Trionfi*. The prisoners of the god of love include Julius Caesar, Cleopatra, Phaedra, Jason, Oenone, Helen, Pyramus and Thisbe, and Lancelot. Then appears Chastity, as Laura, accompanied by such heroines as Penelope and Judith, as well as her shining Virtues, weaponless but defiant: Honor, Shame, Prudence, Temperance, Steadfastness of Soul, and Purity. Laura battles with and triumphs over Cupid, but on her return from Rome and the temple of Chastity, she is met by Death who is attended by a troop of Fortune's minions, erstwhile kings whose riches are now of no avail:

> Wretched they who place their hopes below
> On the poor pageant of this empty show.

Death triumphs over Laura, but she appears in a dream to Petrarch to remind him of Fame, who next arrives upon the scene, accompanied by a procession of famous worthies such as Caesar, Scipio, Nero, Brutus, Hector, Aeneas, Alexander the Great, Judas Maccabaeus, Charlemagne, Plato and Aristotle. "Our tryumphs shal passe our pompes shal decay,"[55] warns

Morley in the *Triumphes,* as first Time triumphs and then Eternity, who instructs the reader to fix all hopes on God. Petrarch and Laura are reunited in Eternity.

In the *trionfi* themselves, the only detailed description of a chariot with a group mounted therein occurs in the Triumph of Love, but such illustrators of the work as the fifteenth-century Florentine engraver,[56] picture all six of the personifications riding in chariots and bearing standard properties: Death as a skeleton in black, Time as a winged old man on crutches, Cupid with his bow, Chastity with a palm and a book, Fame with the sword of Justice or with a trumpet, Eternity as a Glory of the Trinity and angels, with the four Evangelists represented as they were at the chariot of Beatrice, by symbols of a man, lion, eagle, and ox. The other personifications are placed in chariots drawn by emblematic animals—Chastity by a unicorn, Death by buffaloes, Fame by elephants, and Time by stags.

The chariots in which the personifications were seated were the customary classical mounting for triumphing Roman heroes or mythological gods. In mythology, these conveyances were drawn by animals which became symbolically associated with the deities, as Venus' doves and Juno's peacocks. So it is that the aspect of a chariot-drawn personage often leads to association with both the military triumph and the mythological god. Dante, for instance, says that Beatrice's chariot in the Triumph of Revelation outdid not only those of Africanus and Augustus, but that of the sun as well. On the other hand, the *hybris* of a conqueror like Caesar in *Ceasar and Pompey* is revealed by the triumphing hero's attempting to match the glory of Apollo.[57] The many associations of a military triumph with the magnificent chariot of the sun god may reflect the medieval allegorizing of classical myth; allusions to Phaeton, for example, are more than simple analogies, since it will be recalled that Golding regarded Apollo's son as a symbol of blind ambition. Thus joining Petrach's *trionfi* and the public Renaissance allegorical triumphs were the classical gods, as representatives of abstract qualities, as the natural inhabitants of animal-drawn chariots, and as figures to whom an allegorical significance had been attached in the Middle Ages.

Petrarch's *Triumphs* may also suggest the aspect of the pageant as a stage of life, as reflected in the Pageants of Richard Beauchamp and Jaques' seven ages speech.[58] Celebrating the prevailing moods of the various periods of life, the *Trionfi* presents the triumph of age and death over youth and love, and then of the spirit, and finally of Divinity over all. The applicability of this pattern to the life of an individual can be seen in Stephen Hawes' allegorical romance, *The Pasttime of Pleasure*. After completing the first two stages, the hero is arrested by Death, whereupon Fame, in a robe covered with burning tongues, announces that she will spread his renown as she did that of the Nine Worthies. Next, just as in the *Triumphs,* appear Time, in conventional attire, and Eternity, who reminds the reader of the mutability of worldly things.

Individually as well as collectively, the *Triumphs* of Petrarch permeated art, literature, the pageant and the drama. Naturally, some of these allegorical triumphs were more popular than others as themes for shows and plays. In Reformation England, the triumph of Divinity was not given the prominence it received in the Catholic countries. As might be suspected, the Triumph of Love and Triumph of Chastity became immediate and continuing favorites in progress entertainments and later in the masques; the Triumph of Death effectively symbolized the association of the funeral and military triumphs in plays about English and Roman history.

The Triumph of Fortune supplanted or supplemented the medieval Goddess Fortuna and her wheel; the Triumph of Fame with its Nine Worthies was a favorite in city entries, and the Triumph of Time expressed a theme recurrent in the Renaissance.

An entertainment of the Queen in 1578 demonstrates the adaptability of the Triumphs of Love and Chastity to the progress show. Entering triumphantly in his chariot, Cupid encountered Chastity accompanied by her maids, Modesty, Temperance, Good Exercise and Shamefastness. As she did in Petrarch's poem, Chastity reminded the audience that she needed no weapons, since she was armed with thoughts of virtue. She proved the strength of this spiritual armor by throwing Cupid out of his coach and claiming it for her own; thus Chastity triumphed over Desire. Then Chastity, symbolizing the Queen's virtue, commended Elizabeth for having chosen the chaste life, and presented her with Cupid's bow to shoot at whom she pleased, since none could wound her Highness' heart. Prominent in a number of later masques, this sentiment is to be found as well in Oberon's speech in *A Midsummer Night's Dream,*

> But I might see young Cupid's fiery shaft
> Quench'd in the chaste beams of the wat'ry moon,
> And the imperial vot'ress passed on,
> In maiden meditation, fancy-free.   II, i, 161 ff.

On the same progress, another entertainment combined the triumph of Fortune with the love *débat.* "Intended to be played in a garden," the show was concerned with the suit for the hand of Lady Beauty, by Manhood, Favor, and Desert, each of whom pleaded his case before the Queen. Then Good Fortune entered, and the decision was made not on merit, but by a fight, enlivened with shots and "legges and armes of men (well and lively wrought) to be let fall in numbers on the grounde, as bloudy as mighte be." Since "Destinie. . .shal governe all," Good Fortune overthrew the other contestants and marched off in triumph.[59]

Not far removed from the progress entertainments' living depictions of Petrarch's poem is *The Rare Triumphs of Love and Fortune*. In this early play, Venus and Fortune debate their respective influence, and display their conquests in shows offered as *confirmatio*. Introduced with earthy comments by Mercury and Vulcan, these shows exhibit such members of the *Triumphs* as Troilus and Cressida, Dido, and Hero and Leander in Venus' "Triumph of Love," and Alexander the Great, Pompey and Caesar in Fortune's show. In the dramatic framework, the two are ordered by Jupiter to test their power over the principals in the play. Thus the entr'actes colorfully display the successive victory marches, as it is directed "Strike vp Fortunes triumphes with Drummes and Trumpets," or "Strike vp a noise of Viols, Venus Triumphe."[60] At the end of the play, Jupiter resolves the contest by decreeing divided power—those whom Fortune favors, Venus is not to destroy and *vice versa*.

Especially prevalent in dramatic allusion and imagery was the popular triumph of love. It is artistically introduced in *The Tragedie of Caesar and Pompey,* where in the midst of military triumphs, Antony is distracted by Cleopatra's victory over his heart:

> . . .shee triumphes ore my conquered heart,
> In Cupids Chariot ryding in her pride,
> And leades me capitue bounde in Beauties bondes:
>
> III, ii

In *Titus Andronicus,* after Aaron has employed a pageant-like image to describe the Queen's good fortune,[61] he draws from the Triumph of Love to express his own power over Tamora, whom he

>   ... in triumph long
> Hast prisoner held, fett'red in amorous chains.
>   II, i, 14 f.

Shakespeare associates the pageant or triumph with a love which is also artificial and ephemeral. In *A Midsummer Night's Dream,* Puck joyfully exhibits for the King's entertainment a "fond pageant" of four true lovers who, at the application of magic flower juice, veer in their sworn attachments. Similarly, in Book III of *The Faerie Queene,* which also concerns the trials of fond lovers, Spenser remarks, "how diversely Love doth his pageant play."[62] Like Puck, Corin in *As You Like It* exhibits a wooing scene as a "pageant truly play'd". Here the old shepherd leads Rosalind and Celia to behold the archaic and artificial love suit of the devoted Silvius to the hard-hearted Phebe.[63] The most ironic allusion to Cupid's pageant is Troilus' assurance to Cressida that true love is steadfast: "Oh, let my lady apprehend no fear! In all Cupid's pageant there is presented no monster."[64] The idealistic Troilus seems to be referring to the animals which drew Cupid's triumphal chariot, and implying that there was no place for the horned monster that represented the cuckold.

While Petrarch represented the Triumph of Fame as a higher achievement than that of Love, *Love's Labour's Lost* reverses this concept. At the beginning of the play, the heroes dedicate themselves to achieving through scholarship the Triumph of Fame over Time. Later they are converted to fight for the victory of Love: "Saint Cupid then! and, soldiers, to the field!"[65]

The Triumph of Fortune, which is so widely alluded to, is not to be found in the *Trionfi.* However, her victories, as well as those of the Fates, or Fate, were implicit in Petrarch's Triumph of Death, and soon the popular Goddess Fortuna of the Middle Ages took her place in the allegorical triumphs of the Renaissance. The last dumb show in *Jocasta* depicts the triumph of Fortune, who is dressed in white, posed with her feet upon a globe, in a chariot drawn by kings and beggars. In *The Contention between Liberality and Prodigality*, at the beginning of Scene VI, Fortune also enters in her chariot drawn by kings. Sometimes, Fortune's wheel became identified with that of a chariot, as revealed by a lottery verse which accompanied "Fortune's Wheeles" at York House in 1601:

> Fortune must now no more on Triumph ride;
> The wheeles are yours that did her chariots guide.[66]

Triumphing Fortune retained her earlier reputation as a fickle lady who deserted those whom she had formerly favored. In *The Wounds of Civil War*, this image is an appropriate reminder of the vicissitudes of Fate, a theme also expressed in the play by the juxtaposition of the funeral and the triumph:

> The wayward lady of this wicked world,
> That leads in luckless triumph wretched men,
> My Roman friends, hath forced our desires,
>
> II, i

says young Marius, describing the turn of Caius Marius' fortune, who once "Even with a beck commanded Asia." And later, Sylla reflects upon his own downfall:

> The man that made the world to stoope
> And fettered fortune in the chains of power
> Must droop and draw the chariot of Fate
> Along the darksome banks of Acheron.
>
> V, i

Likewise, Wendoll remarks in *A Woman Killed with Kindness*, "the swift fates drag me at their chariot wheel."[67] It is only to be expected that the superman Tamburlaine reverse the procedure and hold "the Fates bound fast in yron chaines."[68]

In the *Henry VI* trilogy and *Richard III*, the Triumph of Fortune is almost a leitmotif in this chronicle of the falls of princes. In 2 *Henry VI*, Eleanor, Duchess of Gloucester, anticipates the favor of Fortune. When she remarks,

> . . .I will not be slack
> To play my part in Fortune's pageant,
>
> I, ii, 66 f.

she is evidently thinking of a show of Fortune's favorites, like that in *The Rare Triumphs of Love and Fortune*. But dramatic irony rings in these words, since Fortune is to advance Eleanor no further, but rather is to cast her down from the height she has attained. Later in the play, in a visual depiction of the fall of pride, the Duchess walks in a gown of penance through streets in which, the Duke recalls, she once rode in triumph.[69]

In the next play in the series, the virago Margaret exultantly triumphs over the captured York, whom she orders exhibited upon a hill, and crowned with a paper crown. York reminds the mocking Queen that the victory is not hers but Fortune's:

> How ill-beseeming is it in thy sex
> To triumph like an Amazonian trull
> Upon their woes whom fortune captivates!
>
> I, iv, 113 ff.

Two acts later, the fickle goddess has triumphed over Margaret. As the former Queen mourns the loss of her throne as a defeat by Fortune, the French King offers stoical advice:

> Yield not thy neck
> To fortune's yoke, but let thy dauntless mind
> Still ride in triumph over all mischance.
>
> III, iii, 16 ff.

Margaret, whose figure threads the tetralogy, recalls the

triumph of Fortune to Elizabeth in *Richard III*. Combining pageant stage, tableau grouping, representation of the ruler and royal family, painting and decoration, Margaret draws an image of Elizabeth as an usurping Queen whose former state was as unreal and ephemeral as a pageant sovereign's:

> I call'd thee then vain flourish of my fortune;
> I call'd thee then poor shadow, painted queen,
> The presentation of but what I was,
> The flattering index of a direful pageant,
> One heav'd a-high to be hurl'd down below,
> A mother only mock'd with two fair babes,
> A dream of what thou wast, a garish flag,
> To be the aim of every dangerous shot;
> A sign of dignity, a breath, a bubble,
> A queen in jest, only to fill the scene.
>
> IV, iv, 82 ff.

Again, as in the Prince's entry in this same play, and as in the imagery of *Coriolanus* and *Hamlet,* Shakespeare is achieving an effective contrast by portraying a somber subject in terms of the splendid entry. Here the festive and optimistic pageant is employed to express the emptiness of Queen Elizabeth's state, which is like the *tableau vivant* presented to the entering ruler, a mere show or "vain flourish" in which an actor represents the real sovereign. So the shadow Elizabeth depicts the fortune of the true Queen, Margaret. Like Margaret, she is "heav'd a-high" and "mock'd" with the two children at her side, since they also are but actors in a street tableau. A mere "flattering index" or prologue to a pageant which proves direful in its enactment, this dream-like display of insubstantial glory soon ends, as do all such shows. The painted Queen is "hurl'd down," after playing "A queen in jest, only to fill the scene."

Thus the Triumph of Fortune develops out of Petrarch's Triumph of Death to become a vivid Renaissance symbol expressing classical and medieval ideas concerning the fickle goddess. As in *The Wounds of Civil War,* sometimes death was the culmination of Fortune's disfavor; sometimes, reflecting the Stoic doctrine, death represented a triumph over the vicissitudes of Fortune in life. Welcoming the joint triumphal and funeral procession in *Titus Andronicus,* Marcus remarks Stoically of those who have died:

> . . . safer triumph is this funeral pomp
> That hath aspir'd to Solon's happiness
> And triumphs over chance in honour's bed.
>
> I, i, 176 ff.

As Housman reminds the young athlete, a Stoical compensation can be derived from thwarting Fortune by death, a sentiment with which Richard consoles himself in *The True Tragedy of Richard III*:

Tho that Fortune hath decreed, to set reuenge with trimphs on my wretched head, yet death . . . hath sworne to make a bargaine for my lasting fame . . .

> xvii, 1975 ff:

In *Ceasar and Pompey,* Brutus similarly dwells on his future fame as recompense for his present death, as he reminds Caesar:

> My mournefull Beere shall winne more Praise and Fame
> Then thy triumphing sun-bright Chariot.
>
> I, ii

Richard and Brutus, in true Renaissance fashion, are concerned not only with thwarting Fortune by death, but with requiting death by "lasting fame."

While the Stoics found compensation in death's triumph over chance, the Triumph of Fortune and Death was answered by the Renaissance with the Triumph of Fame, wherein the great deeds of individuals immortalized them in this

world. As a theme for street shows, Fame's triumph was easily
the most popular of the various *trionfi*. Almost obligatory,
along with the pageants of genealogy and virtues, was an exhibit comparing the honored sovereign with outstanding
historical characters, and promising him even greater fame.
Sometimes the figure of Fame herself promised renown to
the ruler, as at Norwich in 1578. The most popular device
for presenting this theme was the exhibit of the Nine Worthies of history, to whom the ruler was favorably likened.
On occasion, he was elected to membership in this select
group, which was generally comprised of three Pagans, Hector, Alexander and Julius Caesar; three Jews, Joshua, David
and Judas Maccabaeus; and three Christians, Arthur, Charlemagne, and Godfrey of Bouillon. With the expansion and
adaptation characteristic of the street shows, Petrarch greatly
augments the number of worthies in Fame's entourage in the
Triumphs.

The assurance of everlasting fame echoes persistently
through the royal celebrations. Climaxing Jonson's *Masque of
Queens* is the Triumph of Fame, which closes with the following song:

> Force Greatnesse all the glorious wayes
> You can, it soone decayes;
> But so good Fame shall, neuer:
> Her triumphs as theyr Causes, are for euer.[70]

The welcoming orations, as well as the shows, conventionally
prophesied eternal fame for the deserving entrant. But the
tables are turned in *Measure for Measure,* as the entering
Duke voices his concern for the fame of his welcomer, Angelo,
whose merit

> . . . .deserves, with characters of brass,
> A forted residence 'gainst the tooth of time
> And razure of oblivion.   V, i, 11 ff.

THE "INSUBSTANTIAL PAGEANT"

Amid the spectacle, the noise, the excitement of many a celebration, sounded this note of apprehension concerning the "tooth of time." As the sun was setting on the day's festivities, there stretched in shadow behind the decorated arches of Fame, the great black arches of triumpher Time. Then, reflective showmakers and spectators might have shared the perception that the passing show concretely and compactly exemplifies the evanescence of the seemingly lasting beauties of this world. A recurrent theme in sixteenth century literature, the Triumph of Time represented *contemptu mundi* with a difference. Added to the medieval teachings that the beauties of this world were insubstantial and fleeting as compared with the stability of heaven, was the Renaissance regret that such beauty should pass so soon.

One of the best manifestations of this transitory glory was the pageant—a symbol of short-lived beauty celebrating worldly achievement. Many of the men and women of Shakespeare's audience considered brass monuments fairly substantial; they might not have paused to joy in the brief flowering or to lament the passing of a yellow primrose; yet these persons almost daily observed preparations for some pageant or water display or parade. When the day of the celebration arrived, they jostled one another for advantageous positions from which to behold the splendor of the shows and the ruler. After the day of spectacle had passed, these same citizens saw the razing of the structures and the demolition or removal of the decorations. Lamenting the ephemeral magnificence of the pageants prepared for James' entry, the architect Stephen Harrison proposed to preserve them in his book by illustration and description:

Reader, the limmes of these great Triumphall bodies (lately disioynted and taken in sunder) I haue thou seest (for thy sake) set in their apt and right places againe: so that now they are to stand as perpetual monuments, not to be shaken in peeces, or to be broken downe, by the malice of that enuious destroyer of all things, Time.[71]

Ancient Romans and Renaissance English alike found the triumphal arches suggestive of the transitoriness of glory and the certainty of death. Almost invariably associated with the arch, the pageant, with its vividly fixed representations of the universal aspects of the life of man and commonwealth, came to symbolize in its brief beauty the glories of this world and of life itself.[72] Spenser uses the symbol to demonstrate the evanescence of the world's vanities in *A Theatre for Worldlings,* wherein he translates the *Visions* of Petrarch and du Bellay. Here, illustrated by woodcuts, are presented such scenes in the "wide and universal theatre" as a ship, a tree flourishing and then blasted, a spring with muses and nymphs, and the genius of a stream—all recognizable ingredients of the pageants. Of a triumphal arch depicted first in splendor and then in ruins (See Plate VI), Spenser says:

> I saw raisde vp on pillers of Iuorie
> Whereof the bases were of richest golde,
> The chapters Alabaster, Christall frises,
> The double front of a triumphall arke.
> On eche side portraide was a victorie.
> With golden wings in habite of a Nymph.
> And set hie vpon triumphing chaire,
> The auncient glorie of the Romane lordes.
> The worke did shewe it selfe not wrought by man,
> But rather made by his owne skilfull hande
> That forgeth thunder dartes for Ioue his sire.
> Let me no more see faire thing vnder heauen,
> Sith I haue seene so faire a thing as this,
> With sodaine falling broken all to dust.[73]

Later, Spenser uses the same theme and technique in his *Ruines of Time,* where he beholds in a vision "tragicke Pageants," which are devices symbolizing the tyranny of time. The prologue is delivered by the genius of the city, a frequent member of the *tableaux vivants.* Used emblem-like to illustrate the instability of worldly things, many of these "pageants" take such forms common to the street shows as a paradise or bower, a temple, and a giant. All of the devices are represented first in strength and splendor and then in sudden destruction.[74]

In two of his most beautiful and thoughtful passages, Shakespeare employs features of the pageant to express the transience of the glories of this world. In *Antony and Cleopatra,* the once "triple pillar of the world," the giant figure, Antony, likens himself to "black Vesper's pageants," the clouds of evening which assume the shapes of familiar figures and settings of the pageants, but are even more insubstantial:

> Sometime we see a cloud that's dragonish;
> A vapour sometime like a bear or lion,
> A tower'd citadel, a pendent rock,
> A forked mountain, or blue promontory
> With trees upon't that nod unto the world
> And mock our eyes with air. Thou hast seen these signs;
> They are black Vesper's pageants. . . .
> That which is now a horse, even with a thought
> The rack dislimns, and makes it indistinct
> As water is in water. . . .
> My good knave Eros, now thy captain is
> Even such a body. Here I am Antony;
> Yet cannot hold this visible shape, my knave.
>
> IV, xiv, 2 ff.

Prospero wisely sums up the pageant images' rich implications of the beauty of this world and of life and the evanescence of both. He is likening the insubstantial world not only to the show just presented, but also to the pageants in general, whose familiar trappings—the towers, palaces, temples and globe—he uses symbolically, as Spenser did in *The Ruines of Time*. Like the masque just past, like *The Tempest*, like the pageant arches which reproduced in little the world's towers, palaces and temples in their fleeting beauty and swift destruction, so the pageants of man's life and of the "great globe itself" will dissolve and "leave not a rack behind:"

> Our revels now are ended. These our actors,
> As I foretold you, were all spirits and
> Are melted into air, into thin air;
> And, like the baseless fabric of this vision,
> The cloud-capp'd towers, the gorgeous palaces,
> The solemn temples, the great globe itself,
> Yea, all which it inherit, shall dissolve,
> And, like this insubstantial pageant faded,
> Leave not a rack behind.
>
> IV, i, 148 ff.

Notes

NOTES TO CHAPTER ONE

1. John Nichols, *The Progresses, Processions, and Magnificent Festivities of King James the First* (London, 1828), I, 342.

2. George Kernodle, *From Art to Theatre* (Chicago, 1944), pp. 234 f. gives a complete bibliography of accounts of royal entries in England and Scotland, 1189-1661. Representative reports of public festivities during the reigns of Elizabeth and James are to be found in the two works of John Nichols, *The Progresses and Public Processions of Queen Elizabeth* (London, 1823), new ed., 3 vols., and *The Progress . . . of King James*, 4 vols. Pp. 223 ff. below list sources of entertainments referred to in the text.

3. Robert Withington, *English Pageantry* (Cambridge, Mass., 1918-1920), 2 vols., details the history of the street pageants and the royal entries and Lord Mayors' Shows at which they were presented.

4. Sir Nicholas Harris Nicolas, *History of the Battle of Agincourt* (London, 1832), pp. 295 ff. Withington, *op. cit.*, I, 135, n. 3.

5. Kernodle, *op. cit.*, discusses the influence of art on the *tableaux vivants*, the development of the showpieces on which they were staged, and the relationship of this show architecture to the Renaissance stage.

6. Edward Hall, *Hall's Chronicle* (London, 1809), pp. 113 f.

7. Walter W. Greg, *Dramatic Documents from the Elizabethan Playhouses* (Oxford, 1931), pp. 26-28, 125, 165, 170.

8. Philip Henslowe, *Henslowe Papers,* Walter W. Greg, ed. (London, 1907), pp. 114-118, 120 f.

9. As quoted by G. L. Kittredge in his edition of *The Complete Works of William Shakespeare* (Boston, 1936), p. 837. Unless otherwise designated, all references to Shakespeare's plays are to this edition, which all the quoted passages in the text follow.

10. The Malone Society Reprints, xxiii, 1511-1580. These editions hereafter cited as MSR.

11. I, i, 14 ff.

12. Christopher Marlowe, *Works,* C. F. Tucker Brooke, ed. (Oxford, 1925), 11. 592 ff; 633 f. Future references to Marlowe's plays are to this edition.

13. II, i, 179 ff. When the procession prepares to leave the stage, this Herald assumes the services of a whiffler, calling, "Give way there, and go on;" 1. 209.

14. V, v, 1 ff., s.d.

15. III, v, 1 ff.

16. IV, iv, 1 ff; IV, v; IV, vi, 10 ff.

17. *Old English Drama*, Students' Facsimile Edition (Hereafter referred to as OED), CLXX, K4 verso-L verso.

18. 1 *Henry IV*, II, iv, 415 ff.

19. René Schneider, "Le Thème du Triomphe dans les entrées solennelles en France à la Renaissance," *Gazette des beaux-arts*, I (February, 1913), pp. 89-103; Jacob Burckhardt, *The Civilization of the Renaissance in Italy*, tr. S. G. C. Middlemore (Vienna, 1937) pp. 217-219.

20. *The Plays and Poems of Robert Greene*, J. Churton Collins, ed. (Oxford, 1905), vol. 1, I, i, 1 ff. Future references to Greene's plays are to this edition.

21. I, 35:

> O Diva, gratum quae regis Antium
> praesens vel imo tollere de gradu
> mortale corpus vel superbos
> vertere funeribus triumphos.

22. Thomas Newton, ed. (London, 1927), II, 139 f.

23. I, i, 117, 339.

24. II, i, 178 s.d. ff.

25. IV, i, 47.

26. *Four Chapters of North's Plutarch* (facsimile, 1595 edition), F. A. Leo, ed. (London, 1878), p. 247.

27. II, ii, 112-118. See pp. 186 f. below.

28. John Leland, *Antiquarii de Rebus Britannicis Collectanea*, Thomas Hearne ed. (London, 1770), IV, 195.

29. R. W. [ilson], ". . . The Three Lordes and Three Ladies of London . . . ," OED, CXLV, I 2 verso.

30. *The Shakespeare Apocrypha*, C. F. Tucker Brooke ed. (Oxford, 1918), V, 1. 193; 38.

31. III, i, 88.

32. III, ii, 45 f.

33. I, i, 56.

34. I, ii, 1 ff.

35. North, *op. cit.*, p. 784. Shakespeare combines Caesar's triumph with the feast Lupercalia.

36. *Works*, R. W. Bond, ed. (Oxford, 1902), Vol. 2, I, i, 74, 78, 51. Future references to Lyly's plays are to this edition.

37. OED, XXXVI, D 3 verso.

38. *Richard III*, II, ii, 120 ff.

39. III, i, 7 ff. See below, pp. 75 ff.

40. III, iv, 1 ff.

41. V, i, 2.

42. V, ii, 7 ff.

43. *Ben Jonson*, C. H. Herford, P. and E. Simpson, ed. (Oxford 1925-1947), Vol. 3, I, ii, 50 ff. (Except as designated, future references to Jonson's works are to this edition.) The expense account for the Grocers' Pageant for 1617 includes four pounds for the printing of 500 books. Frederick W. Fairholt, *Lord Mayors' Pageants* (London, 1843-1844), Pt. I, Appendix, p. 165.

44. Nichols, *Prog. Eliz.*, I, 39.
45. *Antony and Cleopatra*, II, ii, 216 ff.
46. North, *op. cit.*, p. 1005.
47. P. B 3.
48. P. F 2 verso.
49. 1 *Henry IV*, III, ii, 46 ff.
50. *Edward II*, 1. 959.
51. *King John*, IV, ii, 1 ff.
52. *Richard II*, G. L. Kittredge, ed. (Boston, 1941), p. 178.
53. 1 *Henry IV*, III, ii, 53. This observation is indebted to Prof. Fred Tupper, who first pointed out to the writer the effect in the passage from *Julius Caesar*.
54. *Henry V*, V, Ch. 11.
55. II, i, 283.
56. V, v, 42.
57. As proposed by J. Dover Wilson, ed., with A. Quiller-Couch, *Measure for Measure* (London, 1922), p. 118.
58. *Richard II*, I, iv, 24 ff.
59. *Coriolanus*, II, i, 76 f.

NOTES TO CHAPTER TWO

1. Milton Boone Kennedy, *The Oration in Shakespeare* (Chapel Hill, 1942), pp. 167, 205 f.
2. Nichols, *Prog. Eliz.*, II, 139.
3. Thomas Wilson, *Arte of Rhetorique*, G. H. Mair, ed. (Oxford, 1909), pp. 11-14.
4. George Puttenham, *The Arte of English Poesie*, Gladys D. Willcock and Alice Walker, ed. (Cambridge, 1936), Ch. XVI, p. 35.
5. See below, pp. 157 f.
6. Thomas Nashe, *The Unfortunate Traveller*, Philip Henderson, ed. (London, 1930), pp. 50 f.
7. OED, LXXV, F.
8. Nashe, *op cit.*, pp. 51-54.
9. Nichols, *Prog. Eliz.*, II, 155-159.
10. *Ibid.*, pp. 170 f.
11. *The Pilgrimage to Parnassus*, W. D. Macray, ed. (Oxford, 1886), II, v, 781 ff.
12. IV, iv, 67.
13. Nichols, *Prog. Eliz.*, I, 407.
14. *Ibid.*, II, 96-100.
15. *Two Noble Kinsmen*, III, v, 100 ff; *Love's Labour's Lost*, IV, ii, 58, and cf. Nine Worthies' speeches, V, ii, 555 ff.
16. III, i, 1. E. K. Chambers, *The Elizabethan Stage* (Oxford, 1923), I, 131 f.
17. Nichols, *Prog. Eliz.*, I, 545-547.
18. P. F verso.

19. *Op. cit.,* Ch. XXV, p. 49. *Henry VIII,* V, v, 15 ff.

20. Nichols, *Prog. James,* I, 239.

21. Nichols, *Prog. Eliz.,* II, 165.

22. *Ibid.,* III, 91.

23. *Ibid.,* II, 141 f.

24. *Henry VIII,* V, v, 43.

25. "Prophetae," *Chief Pre-Shakespearean Dramas,* J. Q. Adams, ed. (Boston, 1924), p. 41.

26. Nichols, *Prog. James,* I, 545 n.

27. III, i, 59 f.

28. Nichols, *Prog. Eliz.,* III, 108 f.

29. *Ibid.,* pp. 131 f. For the genesis of the "wild man" see E. K. Chambers, *The Medieval Stage* (Oxford, 1903), I, 185.

30. *The Shakespeare Apocrypha,* III, iii, 50 ff.

31. Nichols, *Prog. Eliz.,* II, 139 ff.

32. *Ibid.,* I, 379.

33. "The Masque in Shakespere's Plays," *Archiv für das Studium der Neueren Sprachen,* CXXV (1910), 71-82.

34. John Stow, *A Survey of London,* C. L. Kingsford, ed. (Oxford, 1908), I, 96.

35. Nichols, *Prog. Eliz.,* III, 570-575.

36. George Chapman, *The Comedies,* Thomas Marc Parrott, ed. (London, 1914), Sc. xiv, 11. 181 ff.

NOTES TO CHAPTER THREE

1. Francis Beaumont and John Fletcher, *Works,* A. Glover and A. R. Waller, eds. (Cambridge, 1908), Vol. 6, IV, i, p. 220.

2. IV, i, 10 f.

3. Leland, *op. cit.,* IV, 190.

4. *The English Works,* W. E. Campbell and A. W. Reed, eds. (New York, 1931), p. 332.

5. Karl Young, *The Drama of the Medieval Church* (Oxford, 1933), I, 90 f.

6. Leland, *op. cit.,* IV, 220.

7. For a history of the development and mechanics of the form see Withington, *op cit,* I; Kernodle, *op. cit.,* pp. 52-108.

8. Nichols, *Prog. Eliz.,* I, 397.

9. P. I 2.

10. Jonson, Vol. 3, I, ii, 29 ff.

11. OED, Vol. LIV, IV, i, p. E4 verso.

12. Stow, *op. cit.,* II, p. 41.

13. John Stow, *A Survey of the Cities of London and Westminster . . .* enlarged by John Strype (London, 1754), I, 16.

14. *Op. cit.,* 130-153.

15. Nichols, *Prog. Eliz.*, I, 50.

16. Adams, *op. cit.*, p. 215.

17. Cf. Dekker's "The Whore of Babylon," *Dramatic Works*, R. H. Shepherd, ed. (London, 1873), Vol. II, p. 218 f., where it is announced that the sea god has set on the shores of England a distressed people, marginally noted as "the Netherlanders." "They haue but 17. daughters young and faire," who wish to wait on the Queen. Future references to Dekker's plays are to this edition.

18. Thomas Dekker, *The Magnificent Entertainment* . . . . , reprinted in Nichols, *Prog. James*, I, 337-376. Stephen Harrison, *The Archs of Triumph erected in honor of : . . Prince James* . . . (London, 1604); B[en]. Jon-[son]: *His Part of King James his Royall . . . Entertainement* . . . , Herford and Simpson, ed. VII, 83-109.

19. See Withington, *op. cit.*, II, 3-28, for a discussion of the development of the Lord Mayor's Show to 1605.

20. I, i, 11.

21. I, iii, 18 f.

22. John Stow, *Annales* (London, 1615), p. 887; Nichols, *Prog. James*, II, 92.

23. Robert Withington, "The Lord Mayor's Show for 1590," Modern Language *Notes*, XXXIII (1918), 8-13; Hugo Shütt, *The Life and Death of Jack Straw* (Heidelberg, 1901), p. 80.

24. Reprinted in *Harleian Miscellany* (London, 1746), VIII, 422-441.

25. Dekker, Vol. 1. I, i, p. 14.

26. III, i, 773 ff. Here the heroine displays to Aeneas pictures of her suitors, whom she, Aeneas, and his companions identify.

27. Dekker, Vol. 1, p. 257: "Enter Tucca, his boy after him with two pictures vnder his cloake, and a wreath of nettles; Horace and Bubo pul'd in by th' hornes bound both like Satyres . . . "

28. *The Works of Mr. William Shakespear*, Nicholas Rowe, ed. (London, 1714), VI, facing p. 301. Wall pictures and miniatures are discussed in the Variorum, I, 290.

29. Withington, *Eng. Pag.*, I, 195 f.

30. Nichols, *Prog. Eliz.*, I, 514.

31. *The Shakespeare Apocrypha*, III, i, 1 ff.

32. Roberta F. Brinkley, *Arthurian Legend in the Seventeenth Century* (Baltimore, 1932); C. B. Millican, *Spenser and the Table Round* (Cambridge, Mass., 1932).

33. Jonson, Vol. 3, I, ii, 78 ff.

34. *The Medieval Heritage of Elizabethan Tragedy* (Berkeley, 1936), p. 352.

35. *Op. cit.*, p. 145.

36. John Webster, "The White Devil," *Complete Works*. F. L. Lucas, ed. (London, 1927), II, ii, 23 ff; 37 ff. (Future references to Webster's plays are to this edition.) *Pericles*, II, Ch. 16 s.d., III, Ch. 14 s.d.

37. F. A. Foster, "The Dumb Show in Elizabethan Drama before 1620," *Englische Studien*, XLIV (1911), 14.

38. J. W. Cunliffe, "Italian Prototypes of the Masque and Dumb Show," *Publications of the Modern Language Association*, XXII (1907), 152.

39. Allardyce Nicoll, *Stuart Masques and the Renaissance Stage* (New York, 1938), pp. 61 f.

40. Ray Heffner, "Spenser's Allegory in Book 1 of 'The Faerie Queene,'" *Studies in Philology*, XXVII (1930), 156-159.

41. Geoffrey Whitney, *Choice of Emblemes*, a facsimile reprint, Henry Green, ed. (London, 1866), p. 321.

42. *Ibid.*, p. A 2 verso.

43. Ben Jonson, *Cynthia Revels*, Alexander C. Judson, ed. (New York, 1912), III, iv, 4 ff.

44. In Rudolph Brotanek, *Die Englischen Maskenspiele* (Vienna, 1902), pp. 309 ff.

45. Cf. *Pericles*, II, ii, 16 ff.

46. T. Tomkins, "Lingua," *Old Plays*, W. C. Hazlitt, ed. (London, 1874), Vol. 9, III, vi, pp. 398 f.

47. I, i, p. A3. Cf. Garden of Plenty Pageant at James' Entry (Plate III).

48. *Ibid.*, III, i, pp. D - D verso; E verso - E 2; H 2 verso.

49. IV, i, 111 ff.

50. I, vi, s.d.; 4 ff.; 21 ff.

51. *Pericles*, V, iii; *Two Noble Kinsmen*, V, i.

52. IV, iv, 915 f.

53. Greene, Vol. 1, II, i, 518 s.d

54. OED, CXLIX, p. D.

55. A. Munday and H. Chettle, "The Death of Robert, Earl of Huntingdon," *Old Plays*, Hazlitt, ed. Vol. 8, V, i and ii, pp. 314 ff.

56. John Marston, *Plays*, H. Harvey Wood, ed. (Edinburgh, 1934-39), Vol. 1, I, ii, 195 f.

57. V, iii, 20.

58. V, i, 171 s.d.

59. V, i, p. G verso.

60. Greene, Vol. 1, II, i, 518.

61. *Troilus and Cressida*, III, iii, 48 f.

62. "The Grief of Joy," *Works*, J. W. Cunliffe, ed. (Cambridge, 1907), II, 526.

63. *English Madrigal Verse*, E. H. Fellowes, ed. (Oxford, 1920), p. 150.

64. Cf. *The Merry Wives of Windsor*, when Ann, as the fairy Queen, instructs the other fairies to write the motto of the Order of the Garter in flowers:

> And *Honi soit qui mal y pense* write
> In em'rald tufts, flow'rs purple, blue, and white,
> Like sapphire, pearl, and rich embroidery,
> Buckled below fair knighthood's bending knee.
> Fairies use flow'rs for their charactery.
>
> V, v, 73 ff.

65. III, iv, 55; III, v.

66. Nichols, *Prog. Eliz.*, III, 101.

67. IV, iii, 40.

68. IV, ii, 58 ff.

69. V, ii, 884. " 'Love's Labour's Lost' Re-Studied," *Studies in Shakespeare, Milton and Donne* (New York, 1925) , p. 18 f.

70. Nichols, *Prog. Eliz.*, III, 110-116. The water-skirmish (p. 115) was popular in medieval festivals and plays, as evidenced in *Robin Hood and the Friar*, Adams, ed. *op. cit.*, 77 ff.

71. Chambers, *Elizabethan Stage*, I, 124; Variorum, pp. 79-91.

72. Nichols, *Prog. Eliz.*, III, 119.

73. II, i, 230 f.

74. Nichols, *Prog. Eliz.*, I, 518-523.

75. J. W. Cunliffe, "The Queenes Majesties Entertainment at Woodstocke," *Publications of the Modern Language Association*, XXVI (1911) , 129 f.

76. *Shakespeare's Ovid*, W. H. D. Rouse, ed. (London, 1904) , p. 16.

77. O. J. Campbell, *Comical Satyre and Shakespeare's "Troilus and Cressida"* (San Marino, 1938) , pp. 83 f.

78. Nichols, *Prog. Eliz.*, III, 498 f.

79. *Ibid.*, I, 502-515.

80. Cunliffe, "The Queenes Majesties Entertainment," comments that the character of Loricus, who was the hermit of the Tale of Hemetes (pp. 93-98) , probably is to be identified with Sir Henry Lee, pp. 138 f. At Quarrendon in 1592 the theme is repeated, as the dying Loricus sends his "living love" to the Queen.

81. Nichols, *Prog. Eliz.*, I, 494.

82. Jonson, Vol. 3, "[the End] Which, in the presentation before Queene E. was thus varyed," ll. 2-29.

83. *Ibid.*, Appendix A, pp. 602 f.

84. Nichols, *Prog. Eliz.*, I, 39.

85. Nichols, *Prog. James*, I, 416 f.

86. I, i, 45 ff.

87. As a member of the King's Company, Shakespeare himself received four and one-half yards of red cloth from the Great Wardrobe for James' coronation festivities in 1604. Chambers, *Eliz. Stage*, II, 211.

88. Cf. above, pp. 56, 72f., 99.

89. "The heavens thee guard and keep, most royal imp of fame!" V, v, 46.

90. IV, vii, 47 ff.

91. Jonson, VII, 90 f.

92. Nichols, *Prog. Eliz.*, I, 441-446.

93. Chambers, *Med. Stage*, I, Ch. VIII, 160-227, discusses the origins and development of folk dances.

94. II, iii, 40 f; III, v, s.d; 95.

95. Another element of the progress entertainment is reflected in the final scene of *The Winter's Tale*, in the metamorphosis of the "statue" of Hermione (cf. Pygmalion's image, *Metamorphoses* X 243 ff.)

96. IV, iv, 379 ff.

97. Nichols, *Prog. Eliz.*, III, 115. At the morris dance at Althorp, just mentioned, the speaker could not be heard "by reason of the throng of the countrey that came in." Jonson, VII, 128.

98. III, i.

99. Cf. Rafe's speech in *The Knight of the Burning Pestle,* above, p. 87. It is to be noted too, that the oft-censured prologues of Time in *The Winter's Tale,* which have been defended by G. L. Kittredge, are similarly couched in the galloping couplets and forced rimes which a figure of Time in the street shows would invariably employ.

100. V, ii, 895 ff.

101. *Medieval Stage,* I, 79-81; 187 f.

102. V, ii, 941 f.

103. Sc. xiv, 1. 220.

104. Dekker, III, 289-294.

NOTES TO CHAPTER FOUR

1. IV, i, 148 ff.

2. Variorum, p. 212.

3. *The Court Masque,* (Cambridge, 1927), p. 342.

4. *Op. cit.,* p. 19 ff.

5. Edmund Spenser, *The Faerie Queene,* V. xiv, 28.

6. *Op. cit.,* pp. 979 f.

7. III, vi, 38 ff.

8. V, ii, 228.

9. I, i, 9.

10. Douce, in the Variorum, p. 4.

11. Fairholt, *op. cit.,* pp. xvi-xx.

12. Vol. 2, p. 235.

13. I, iii, 18 f.

14. *Macbeth,* II, i, 42.

15. Fairholt, *op. cit.,* p. xxi.

16. Henry Machyn, *Diary* (London, 1848), pp. 33, 201, and *passim.*

17. F. W. Fairholt, *Gog and Magog, the Giants in Guildhall* (London, 1859), pp. 11-20.

18. Withington, *Eng. Pag.,* I, 37-47; 50 ff.

19. *Op. cit.,* p. 153.

20. Marston, Vol. 2, III, i, p. 101.

21. Nichols, *Prog. Eliz.,* I, 490.

22. George Chapman, *Bussy D'Ambois,* F. S. Boas, ed. (Boston, 1905), III, i, 118; III, ii, 145; I, i, 6 ff. (cf. *Julius Caesar,* I, ii, 135 f.); V, iv, 97 f.

23. Walter Whiter, *A Specimen of a Commentary on Shakespeare* (London, 1794), pp. 190-193.

24. Fairholt, *Gog and Magog,* p. 65.

25. Illustrations of a number of these personified abstractions can be found in Allan Gilbert's interesting study, *The Symbolic Persons in the Masques of Ben Jonson* (Durham, 1948).

26. Dekker, Vol. 2, pp. 207, 212.

27. *Richard III*, V, v, 33 f.

28. William Herbert, *The History of the Twelve Great Livery Companies of London* (London, 1837), I, 209 f; II, 3, 122.

29. *Cornu-Copiae, Pasquils Night-cap* (London, 1612), p. H.

30. *Shakespeare's Imagery* (New York, 1935), pp. 217 f, 219ff.

31. Cf. Dekker's use in *Old Fortunatus* (Vol. 1, p. 104 f.) of two similar properties to represent the trees of vice and virtue.

32. MSR, 1. 1688, p. G 2 verso.

33. Dekker, Vol. 2, p. 212.

34. II, i, 42, 46.

35. V, ii, 59 f.

36. II, iv, 30.

37. IV, vi, 1 ff.

38. IV, iii, 13 ff.

39. I, ii. 129 f; II, ii, 310 f; III, i, 84 f; III, i, 112 f; III, iv, 154; IV, iv, 38 f.

40. IV, iii, 32 f.

41. II, i, 174 ff.

42. Johnson: "The cries of the slaughter'd regularly followed his motion, as music and a dancer accompany each other." Variorum, p. 236.

43. V, vi, 69 ff.

44. Roger Ascham, *The Scholemaster* (London, 1743), James Upton, ed. p. 89.

45. [Victor Masséna], Prince D'Essling, and Eugène Müntz, *Pétrarque: ses Études D'Art* (Paris, 1902), discuss the influence of *The Triumphs* upon art, pp. 102 ff. Veneziano's "Triumph of Death," facing p. 187. Lorenzo Costa, "Le Triomphe de la Renomée," reprod. in Adolfo Venturi's "Les *Triomphes* de Pétrarque dans l'art Représentatif," *La Revue de l'art ancien et moderne,* XX (1906), facing p. 214.

46. Ernest Law, *The History of Hampton Court Palace* (London, 1885), I, 63 ff.

47. Andres de Almansa y Mendoza, *Two Royall Entertainments* . . . (London, 1623), p. 7.

48. Burckhardt, *op. cit.,* p. 217; plate 274.

49. Nichols, *Prog. Eliz.,* III, 134.

50. *Richard II*, V, ii, 52.

51. Burckhardt, *op. cit.,* pp. 211, 218.

52. Dante, "Purgatorio," *The Divine Comedy* (New York, 1932), Ch. XXIX, pp. 365-369.

53. St. III, pp. 246 f.

54. Lucretius, *Of the Nature of Things,* W. E. Leonard, tr. (London, 1921), Book II, p. 67.

55. *The Triumphes of Petrarch,* Henry Parker, Lord Morley, tr., 1554 (London, 1887), p. 91.

56. See illustrations in *The Triumphs of Francesco Petrarch,* Henry Boyd, tr. (Boston, 1906).

57. OED, XI, III, i, p. E 2.

58. See above, p. 88 f.
59. Nichols, *Prog. Eliz.*, II, 200.
60. MSR, 11. 219-243; 558; 968.
61. See above, p. 168 f.
62. V, i, 2.
63. III, iv, 55; III, V. See above, p. 138.
64. *Troilus and Cressida*, III, ii, 80 f.
65. I, i, I ff; IV, iii, 366.
66. Nichols, *Prog. Eliz.*, III, 571.
67. *Old Plays*, Robert Dodsley, ed. (London, 1825), Vol. 7, p. 245.
68. *Tamburlaine*, Pt. 1, I, ii, 369.
69. II, iv, 13 f.
70. Jonson, VII, 301-316.
71. Stephen Harrison, *op. cit.*, p. K 1.
72. The *Oxford English Dictionary* points out that the word "pageant" was used as early as 1380 to designate "the part acted or played by anyone . . . in the drama of life." Such usage, as well as connection with the *ubi sunt* motif can be seen in Skelton's "Elegy on Edward IV," where Edward lists former worthies, wonders "where are they now," and says of himself,

> Now I sleep in dust,
> I have played my pageant.

73. Edmund Spenser, *Minor Poems*, Ernest de Sélincourt, ed. (Oxford, 1910), p. 493.
74. *Ibid.*, pp. 128 ff; 11. 36; 490 ff.

Bibliography

Adams, Joseph Quincy, *Chief Pre-Shakespearean Dramas*, Boston, Houghton Mifflin Co., 1924.

Almansa y Mendoza, Andres de, *Two Royall Entertainments Lately Given to . . . Prince Charles . . . translated out of the Spanish Originals*, London, 1623.

Arber, Edward, *An English Garner*, 8 vols., Westminster, A. Constable & Co., 1880-97.

Ascham, Roger, *The Scholemaster*, James Upton, ed. London, W. Innys, 1743.

Beaumont, Francis, and John Fletcher, *Works*, A. Glover and A. R. Waller, eds. 10 vols., Cambridge, Univ. Press, 1905-12.

Breton, Nicholas, *Cornu-copiae, Pasquils Night-cap*, London, for T. Thorp, 1612.

Brinkley, Roberta F., *Arthurian Legend in the Seventeenth Century*, Baltimore, Johns Hopkins Press, 1932.

Brooke, C. F. Tucker, ed., *The Shakespeare Apocrypha*, Oxford, the Clarendon Press, 1918.

Brotanek, Rudolph, *Die Englischen Maskenspiele*, Vienna, W. Braumüller, 1902.

Burckhardt, Jacob, *The Civilization of the Renaissance in Italy*, tr. S. G. C. Middlemore, Vienna, the Phaidon Press, [1937].

"Caesar and Pompey, the Tragedie of," anon. (London, 1607), *Old English Drama*, Students' Facsimile Edition, XI, 1913.

Campbell, Oscar James, *Comicall Satyre and Shakespeare's 'Troilus and Cressida,'* San Marino, Huntington Library Publ., 1938.

"Love's Labour's Lost Re-Studied," *Studies in Shakespeare, Milton and Donne*, University of Michigan Publ., New York, Macmillan Co., 1925, pp. 3-45.

Chambers, E. K., *The Elizabethan Stage*, 4 vols., Oxford, the Clarendon Press, 1923.

The Medieval Stage, 2 vols., Oxford, the Clarendon Press, 1903.

Chapman, George, *Bussy D'Ambois*, Frederick S. Boas, ed. Belles Lettres Series, Boston, D. C. Heath & Co., 1905.

The Comedies, Thomas Marc Parrott, ed. London, George Routledge & Sons, 1914.

Cunliffe, John W., "Italian Prototypes of the Masque and Dumb Show," *Publications of the Modern Language Assoc.*, XXII (1907), 140-156.

"The Masque in Shakspere's Plays," *Archiv für das Studium der Neueren Sprachen*, CXXV (1910), 71-82.

"The Queenes Majesties Entertainment at Woodstocke," *Publications of the Modern Language Assoc.*, XXVI (1911), 92-141.

Daniel, Samuel, *Complete Works*, Alexander B. Grosart, ed. 5 vols., London Hazell, Watson and Viney, Ltd., 1885-1896.

Dante Alighieri, *The Divine Comedy*, Carlyle-Wicksteed, tr. New York, Random House, 1932.

Dekker, Thomas, *The Dramatic Works*, R. H. Shepherd, ed. 4 vols., London, John Pearson, 1873.

"The Faire Maide of Bristow," anon. (London, 1605), *Old English Drama*, Students' Facsimile Edition, XXXVI, 1912.

Fairholt, Frederick W., *Gog and Magog, the Giants in Guildhall*, London, John Camden Hotten, 1859.

Lord Mayors' Pageants, 2 pts., London, the Percy Society, 1843-1844.

Farnham, Willard, *The Medieval Heritage of Elizabethan Tragedy*, Berkeley, Univ. of California Press, 1936.

Fellowes, E. H., ed., *English Madrigal Verse*, Oxford, the Clarendon Press, 1920.

Foster, F. A., "The Dumb Show in Elizabethan Drama before 1620," *Englische Studien*, XLIV (1911), 8-17.

Gascoigne, George, *Complete Works*, J. W. Cunliffe, ed. 2 vols., Cambridge, Univ. Press, 1907-10.

Gilbert, Allan, *The Symbolic Persons in the Masques of Ben Jonson*, Durham, Duke Univ. Press, 1948.

Greene, Robert, *The Plays and Poems*, J. Churton Collins, ed. 2 vols., Oxford, The Claredon Press, 1905.

Greg, Walter W., *Dramatic Documents from the Elizabethan Playhouses*, Oxford, The Clarendon Press, 1931.

Hall, Edward, *Hall's Chronicle*, London, Printed for J. Johnson [etc.], 1809.

Harleian Miscellany, 8 vols., London, printed for T. Osborne, 1744-1746.

Harrison, Stephen, *The Archs of Triumph erected in honor of the High and Mighty Prince James* . . . . Invented and published by Stephen Harrison, London, 1604.

Heffner, Ray, "Spenser's Allegory in Book I of 'The Faerie Queene,'" *Studies in Philology*, XXVII (1930), 142-161.

Henslowe, Philip, *Henslowe Papers*, Walter W. Greg, ed. London, A. H. Bullen, 1907.

Herbert, William, *The History of the Twelve Great Livery Companies of London*, 2 vols., London, publ. by the author, 1837.

Heywood, Thomas, "If You Know Not Me, You Know Nobody," Parts I and II (London, 1605-1606), The Malone Society Reprints, Oxford Univ. Press, 1934-1935.

"A Woman Kill'd With Kindness," *Old Plays*, Robert Dodsley, ed. VII, London, Septimus Prowett, 1825.

Jack Straw, the Life and Death of, Hugo Schütt, ed. Heidelberg, C. Winter, 1901.

Jonson, Ben, *Ben Jonson,* C. H. Herford and Percy and Evelyn Simpson, eds. 8 vols., Oxford, the Clarendon Press, 1925-1947.

Cynthia's Revels, Alexander C. Judson, ed. New York, Henry Holt & Co., 1912.

Kennedy, Milton Boone, *The Oration in Shakespeare,* Chapel Hill, Univ. of North Carolina Press, 1942.

Kernodle, George R., *From Art to Theatre,* Chicago, Univ. of Chicago Press, 1944.

"A Knacke to Knowe a Knaue . . ." anon. (London, 1594), *Old English Drama,* Students' Facsimile Edition, LXXV, 1911.

Law, Ernest, *The History of Hampton Court Palace,* 3 vols., London, George Bell & Sons, 1885-1891.

Leland, John, *Antiquarii de Rebus Britannicis Collectanea,* notes by Thomas Hearne, 6 vols., London, Gvl. & J. Richardson, 1770.

Lodge, Thomas, "The Wounds of Civil War, "*Old Plays,* Robert Dodsley, ed. VIII, London, Septimus Prowett, 1825.

Lucretius Carus, Titus, *Of the Nature of Things,* W. E. Leonard. tr. London, J. M. Dent & Sons Ltd., 1921.

Lyly, John, *Complete Works,* R. Warwick Bond, ed. 3 vols., Oxford, the Clarendon Press, 1902.

Machyn, Henry, *Diary,* John Gough Nichols, ed. London, J. B. Nichols, 1848.

Marlowe, Christopher, *Works,* C. F. Tucker Brooke, ed. Oxford, the Clarendon Press, 1925.

Marston, John, *Plays,* H. Harvey Wood., ed. 3 vols., Edinburgh, Oliver and Boyd, 1934-1939.

"Histrio-Mastix" (London, 1610), *Old English Drama,* Students' Facsimile Ed., LIV, 1912.

[Masséna, Victor.] Prince d' Essling and Eugène Müntz, *Pétrarque: ses Études D'Art,* Paris, Gazette des beaux arts, 1902.

Millican, C. B.., *Spenser and the Table Round,* Cambridge, Mass., Harvard Univ. Press, 1932.

More, Thomas, *The English Works,* reprod. in facsimile from William Rastell's ed. of 1557, W. E. Campbell and A. W. Reed, eds. New York, the Dial Press, 1931.

Munday, Anthony [and Henry Chettle], "The Death of Robert, Earl of Huntingdon," *Old English Plays,* Robert Dodsley, ed. new notes by W. Carew Hazlitt, 4th ed., VIII, London, Reeves & Turner, 1874.

"John a Kent & John a Cumber," The Malone Society Reprints, Oxford Univ. Press, 1923.

Nashe, Thomas, *The Unfortunate Traveller,* Philip Henderson, ed. London, The Verona Society, 1930.

Nichols, John, *The Progresses and Public Processions of Queen Elizabeth,* 3 vols., new ed., London, J. B. Nichols, 1823.

The Progresses, Processions, and Magnificent Festivities of King James the First, 4 vols., London, J. B. Nichols, 1828.

Nichols, John Gough, *London Pageants,* London, J. B. Nichols and Son, 1837.

Nicolas, Nicholas Harris, *History of the Battle of Agincourt*, London, 2nd. ed., Johnson & Co., 1832.

Nicoll, Allardyce, *Stuart Masques and the Renaissance Stage*, New York, Harcourt Brace, 1938.

Ovidius Naso, Publius, *Shakespeare's Ovid: being Arthur Golding's Translation of 'The Metamorphoses'*, W. H. D. Rouse, ed. London, the De la More Press, 1904.

The Pageants of Richard Beauchamp, Earl of Warwick, Oxford, The Roxburghe Club, 1908.

Peele, George, *The Arraignment of Paris* (London, 1584), The Malone Society Reprints, Oxford Univ. Press, 1910.

King Edward the First (London, 1593), The Malone Society Reprints, Oxford Univ. Press, 1907.

The Love of King David and Fair Bethsabe (London, 1599), The Malone Society Reprints, Oxford Univ. Press, 1912.

Petrarca, Francesco, *The Triumphs*, Henry Boyd, tr. Boston, Little, Brown & Co., 1906.

The Triumphes of Petrarch, Henry Parker, Lord Morley tr. reprinted by the Roxburghe Club, London, Nichols and Sons, 1887.

The Pilgrimage to Parnassus, W. D. Macray, ed. Oxford, the Clarendon Press, 1886.

Plutarchus, *Four Chapters of North's Plutarch* (facsimile, 1595 ed.), F. A. Leo, ed. London, Trubner & Co., 1878.

Puttenham, George, *The Arte of English Poesie*, Gladys D. Willcock and Alice Walker, eds. Cambridge, the University Press, 1936.

The Rare Triumphs of Love and Fortune, anon. (London, 1589), The Malone Society Reprints, Oxford Univ. Press, 1930.

Rowley, Samuel, "When You See Me You Know Me" (London, 1605), *Old English Drama*, Students' Facsimile Edition, CLXX, 1912.

Schneider, René,"Le Thème du Triomphe dans les entrèes solennelles en France à la Renaissance," *Gazette des beaux-arts*, I (February, 1913), 85-106.

Seneca, Lucius Annaeus, *Seneca, His Tenne Tragedies*, Thomas Newton, ed. (1581), 2 vols., London, Constable & Co., 1927.

Shakespeare, William, *Variorum Shakespeare*, Horace Howard Furness, et. al., eds. 25 vols., Philadelphia, J. B. Lippincott Co., 1871-1944.

Complete Works, George Lyman Kittredge, ed. Boston, Ginn and Co., 1936.

Works, Nicholas Rowe, ed. 7 vols., 3rd ed., London, Jacob Tonson, 1714.

Works, A. Quiller-Couch and J. Dover Wilson, eds. 22 vols., Cambridge, the University Press, 1921-1948.

Spenser, Edmund, *The Faerie Queene*, J. C. Smith, ed. 2 vols., Oxford, the Clarendon Press, 1909.

Minor Poems, Ernest de Sélincourt, ed. Oxford, the Clarendon Press, 1910.

Spurgeon, Caroline F. E., *Shakespeare's Imagery*, New York, Macmillan Co., 1935.

Stow, John, *The Annales,* "continued and augmented" by Edmond Howes, London, Thomas Adams, 1615.

    A Survey of the Cities of London and Westminster . . . "corrected . . . and . . . enlarged" by John Strype, 2 vols., 6th ed. London, Printed for W. Innys [etc.], 1754-1755.

    A Survey of London, C. L. Kingsford, ed. 2 vols., Oxford, the Clarendon Press, 1908.

[Tomkins, T.], "Lingua," *Old English Plays,* Robert Dodsley, ed. new notes by W. Carew Hazlitt, 4th ed., IX, London, Reeves & Turner, 1874.

"The True Tragedy of Richard the Third," anon. (London, 1594), The Malone Society Reprints, Oxford Univ. Press, 1929.

"The Tryall of Cheualry," anon. (London, 1605), *Old English Drama,* Students' Facsimile Ed., CXLIX, 1912.

Venturi, Adolfo, *Les Triomphes* de Pètrarque dans l'art Représentatif," *La Revue de l'art ancien et moderne,* XX (1906), 209-221 (C. G. Picavet, tr.)

Webster, John, *Complete Works,* F. L. Lucas, ed. 4 vols., London, Chatto and Windus, 1927.

Welsford, Enid, *The Court Masque,* Cambridge, the University Press, 1927.

Whetstone, George, ". . . Promos and Cassandra" (London, 1578), *Old English Drama,* Students' Facsimile Edition, CXVII, 1912.

Whiter, Walter, *A Specimen of a Commentary on Shakespeare,* London, T. Cadell, 1794.

Whitney, Geoffrey, *Choice of Emblemes,* (1586) facsimile reprint, Henry Green. ed. London, Lovell Reeve & Co., 1866.

W[ilson], R., ". . . The Three Lordes and Three Ladies of London" (London, 1590), *Old English Drama,* Students' Facsimile Edition, CXLV, 1912.

Wilson, Thomas, *Arte of Rhetorique,* G. R. Mair, ed. Oxford, the Clarendon Press, 1909.

Withington, Robert, *English Pageantry,* 2 vols., Cambridge, Mass., Harvard University Press, 1918-20.

    "The Lord Mayor's Show for 1590," *Modern Language Notes,* XXXIII (1918), 8-13.

Young, Karl, *The Drama of the Medieval Church,* 2 vols., Oxford, the Clarendon Press, 1933.

Appendix

ACCOUNTS OF ROYAL CELEBRATIONS
REFERRED TO IN THE TEXT

1298 Edward I's victory at Falkirk, triumphal celebration at London. Robert Withington, *English Pageantry* (Cambridge, Mass., 1918), I, 124.

1377 Richard II at London, coronation parade. John Gough Nichols, *London Pageants* (London, 1837), p. 11.

1415 Henry V's victory at Agincourt, triumphal entry to London. Sir Nicholas Harris Nicolas, *History of the Battle of Agincourt* (London, 1832), pp. 149-156; 292-300; 325-329. Withington, *op cit.*, I, 132-135.

1431-32 Henry VI at Paris and London, coronation celebration. Withington, *op. cit.*, I, 138-147. J. G. Nichols, *op. cit.*, pp. 18-20: William Herbert, *The History of the Twelve Great Livery Companies of London* (London, 1837), I, 93 f.

1486 Henry VII on progress "towards the North Parties." John Leland, *Antiquarii de Rebus Britannicis Collectanea* (London, 1770), IV, 185-203.

1487 Queen Elizabeth at London for coronation. *Ibid.*, IV, 216-233.

1501 Prince Arthur and Catherine of Aragon at London, marriage celebration. J. G. Nichols, *op. cit.*, pp. 26-33.

1503 Margaret of England and James IV of Scotland at Edinburgh, marriage celebration. Leland, *op. cit.*, IV, 258-300.

1522 Charles V's reception at London. Edward Hall, *Hall's Chronicle* (London, 1809), pp. 637-640.

1533 Anne Boleyn at London for coronation. *Ibid.*, pp. 800-803. Edward Arber, *An English Garner* (London, 1879), II, 41 f.

1546-7 Edward VI at London for coronation. Leland, *op. cit.*, 310-333.

1553 Mary at London for coronation. J. G. Nichols, *op. cit.*, pp. 50-52. Withington, *op. cit.*, I, 188 f.

1554 Reception of King Philip at London. Withington, *op. cit.*, I, 189-194.

1558 Elizabeth's coronation at London. "The Passage of our most drad Soveraigne Lady Quene Elyzabeth through the Citie of London . . ." (London, 1558), reprinted in J. Nichols, *The Progresses and Public Processions of Queen Elizabeth* (London, 1823), I, 38-60.

1572 Elizabeth at Warwick on Progress. *The Black Book*, MS, Corporation of Warwick, in Nichols, *Prog. Eliz.*, I, 309-320.

1573 Elizabeth at Orpington on Progress, John Philipot, *Villare Cantianum,* quoted in Nichols, *Prog. Eliz.,* I, 332.

1573 Elizabeth at Sandwich on Progress. MS account reprinted in Nichols, *Prog. Eliz.,* I, 337-339.

1574 Elizabeth at Bristol on Progress. Thomas Churchyard, "The Whole Order howe . . . Queene Elizabeth was receyved into the Citie of Bristowe" (London, 1575), reprinted in Nichols, *Prog. Eliz.,* I, 393-406.

1575 Elizabeth at Woodstock on Progress. "The Queenes Majesties Entertainment at Woodstocke," J. W. Cunliffe, *Publications of the Modern Language Association,* XXVI (1911), 92-141.

1575 Elizabeth at Kenilworth on Progress. Robert Laneham, "A Letter: Whearin, part of the Entertainment, untoo the Queenz Maiesty, at Killingworth Castl . . . iz signified:" (London, n.d.), Nichols, *Prog. Eliz.,* I, 420-484. George Gascoigne, "The Princely Pleasures at the Courte at Kenelwoorth," (London, 1575), Nichols, *Prog. Eliz.,* I, 485-523.

1575 Elizabeth at Worcester on Progress, the Chamber Order Book, Worcester, Nichols, *Prog. Eliz.,* I, 545-551.

1578 Elizabeth at Wanstead on Progress. Sir Philip Sidney, "The Lady of May," Nichols, *Prog. Eliz.,* II, 94-103.

1578 Elizabeth at Norwich on Progress. B. G., "The joyfull Receyving of the Queene's Majestie into . . . Norwich," (London, n.d.), Nichols, *Prog. Eliz.,* II, 136-178.

1578 Elizabeth at Suffolk and Norfolk on Progress. Thomas Churchyard, "A Discourse of the Queenes Majestie's Entertainment . . ." (London, n.d.), Nichols, *Prog. Eliz.,* II, 179-215.

1581 Entertainment of the French Ambassadors at London. H. Goldwell, "A briefe Declaration of the Shews, Devices, Speeches, and Inventions, done . . . before the Queene's Majestie and the French Ambassadours . . ." (London, 1581), Nichols, *Prog. Eliz.,* II, 310-329.

1581-2 The Duke of Anjou at Antwerp. "The Roiall Interteinement of . . . Prince, Francis . . ," Nichols, *Prog. Eliz.,* II, 354-381.

1588 England's victory over the Armada, triumph at London. Nichols, *Prog. Eliz.,* II, 538-42.

1590 Lord Mayor's Show at London. T. Nelson, Fishmongers' Show for John Allot. Hugo Schütt, *The Life and Death of Jack Straw* (Heidelberg, 1901), Anhang 1, "Ein pageant beim Lordmayor-show im jahre 1590," pp. 80-86.

1591 Lord Mayor's Show at London. George Peele, "Descensus Astraeae," F. W. Fairholt, *Lord Mayors' Pageants* (London, 1843-44), Pt. 1, pp. 27-29.

1591 Elizabeth at Cowdray on Progress. "The Honorable Entertainment given to her Majestie in Progresse, at Cowdray . . . by . . . the Lord Montecute" (London, 1591), Nichols, *Prog. Eliz.,* III, 90-96.

1591 Elizabeth at Elvetham on Progress. "The Honorable Entertainment gieven to the Quene's Majestie, in Progresse, at Elvetham . . . by the

. . . Earle of Hertford," (London, 1591), 2 eds., Nichols, *Prog. Eliz.,* III, 101-121.

1592 Elizabeth at Oxford on Progress. Account by Anthony Wood, *Annals,* reprinted in Nichols, *Prog. Eliz.,* III, 144-148.

1592 Elizabeth at Bisham, Sudley, Rycote, on Progress. "Speeches delivered to her Majestie . . . at . . . Lady Russel's at Bissam . . . the Lorde Chandos at Sudeley; and . . . the Lord Norris's at Ricorte." Nichols, *Prog. Eliz.,* III, 130-143; 168-172.

1592 Elizabeth at Quarrendon on Progress. "Masques performed before Queen Elizabeth." MS printed in Nichols, *Prog Eliz.,* III, 195-213.

1594 Henry IV at Paris, coronation celebration. "The Order of ceremonies obseuered in the annointing and Coronation of the most Christian King of France and Nauarre, Henry the IIII . . . on Sunday the 27 of February 1594." translated from the French by E. A. (London, n.d.)

1596 Entry of Henry IV to Rouen, and presentation of the Order of the Garter. William Segar's account, Nichols, *Prog. Eliz.,* III, 398-407.

1601 Elizabeth at York House. "A Lottery, presented before the Queenes Majestie at York House," Davidson's *Poetical Rapsodie,* (1611), pp. 1-7, reprinted in Nichols, *Prog. Eliz.,* III, 570-575.

1602 Elizabeth at Harefield. "Entertainment of Queen Elizabeth at Harefield, by the Lord Keeper Egerton and the Countess of Derby," MS, in Nichols, *Prog. Eliz.,* III, 586-595.

1603-4 James I at London, coronation celebration. Thomas Dekker, "The Magnificent Entertainment Given to King James . . ." (London, 1604), reprinted in Nichols, *The Progresses, Processions, and Magnificent Festivities of King James the First* (London, 1828), I, 337-376. Stephen Harrison, *The Archs of Triumph erected in honor of the High and Mighty Prince James* (London, 1604).
B[en]. Jon[son]:"His Part of King James his Royall . . . Entertainement . . ." (London, 1604), *Ben Jonson,* ed C. H. Herford, Percy and Evelyn Simpson (Oxford, 1941), VII, 83-109. Reprinted in Nichols *Prog. James,* I, 377-399. Henry Petowe, "England's Caesar," (London, 1603), Nichols, *Prog. James,* I, 235-244.

1603 Queen Ann and Prince Henry at Althorp on Progress. Ben Jonson, "A Particvlar Entertainment of the Qveene and Prince . . . to Althrope, at the . . . Lord Spencers . . ," (London, 1604, Herford and Simpson, VII, 119-131.

1605 James at Oxford on Progress. Matthew Gwynne, entertainment, published with Latin play, "Vertumnus," performed during visit (London, 1607). Reprinted in Nichols, *Prog James,* I, 545 n.

1606 King Christian of Denmark's visit to London. John Stow, *Annales* (London, 1615), p. 887. Letter from John Pory to Sir Robert Cotton, in Nichols, *Prog. James,* II, 91-93.

1612 Lord Mayor's Show at London. Thomas Dekker, "Troia-Nova Triumphans," Fairholt, *Lord Mayors' Pageants,* Pt. 2, pp. 7-32.

1616 Lord Mayor's Show at London. Fishmongers' Pageant. Herbert, *op. cit.,* I, 209 f.

1623 Prince Charles' visit to Spain. Andres de Almansa y Mendoza, *Two Royall Entertainments, Lately Given to the most Illvstrivos Prince Charles* ... Translated out of the Spanish originals ... (London, 1623).

Index